LONDON FIELDS

A JOURNEY THROUGH FOOTBALL'S METROLAND

CHARLIE CONNELLY

LONDON FIELDS

LONDON FIELDS

A JOURNEY THROUGH FOOTBALL'S METROLAND

CHARLIE CONNELLY

MAINSTREAM
PUBLISHING

EDINBURGH AND LONDON

Photographs © Sarah Williams

First published in Great Britain in 1999 by
MAINSTREAM PUBLISHING COMPANY (EDINBURGH) LTD
7 Albany Street
Edinburgh EH1 3UG

ISBN 1 84018 158 3

A catalogue record for this book is available from the British Library

Typeset in Berkeley Book
Printed and bound in Finland by WSOY

Contents

Acknowledgements

Without whom . . .

Tim Bennett, Dominic O'Reilly, the Sands family, the Connelly family, Amanda Collins, Cathy Mineards, Paul s'Jacob, Emma Harvey, the Bahir Dar branch of the Leyton Orient Supporters' Club, Sid Griffin, Pat McGarvey, Heverage the Beverage, all at The Coach and Horses, Pete Howls, Lawrence and Wishart, Mark Perryman, Andy Lopata and other assorted members of the Society of Damn Fine People.

Extra thanks to Sarah Williams, Muswell Hill's finest photographer, for her excellent photography and cheerful support whilst being dragged around some of the capital's footballing backwaters. Now bring on Europe . . .

Special thanks and lots of love to Katie, soon to be wife and Charlton Athletic season-ticket holder (although not necessarily in that order), for putting up with another few months of lonely weekends. As usual, I couldn't have done it without you.

Summer in the City

Introduction

As I stand pressed against the moist armpit of a sweaty accountant, the Northern Line train screeches noisily to a halt at King's Cross. The doors crash open to disgorge a perspiring horde of commuters on to the platform. The throng surges towards the exit, away from the fetid atmosphere and curious warm winds of the underground and on to the suburban trains that will return the collection of bankers, marketing executives, insurance brokers and accountants to their flimsily constructed mock-Tudor houses in the capital's satellite towns.

Swept along in this tide of humanity, a heaving throng of suits and briefcases topped with sweat-beaded foreheads and anxious expressions, I glance back at the train into which another gaggle of office workers is now stuffing itself. As the doors close I see a flash of colour amongst the grey pressed against the glass of the door. Framed by the window is the back of a bright yellow shirt with a large green figure nine. Above the number the legend. 'Ronaldo'.

Barely two weeks have passed since a lacklustre Brazil capitulated to a fluid French side in the World Cup final, held in a Paris now just three hours away by Eurostar. The posters bearing moody black-and-white shots of World Cup stars have all come down, the journalists have come home and the shelves of newsagents are teeming with World Cup reviews, all promising every game, every goal. We've seen the last of Skinner and Baddiel for a while. Hopefully. And Brian Moore has shouted 'It's in there!' for the last time.

Two weeks after the World Cup final, summer sports have finally got a look in. Wimbledon came and went with barely a whimper. The progress of Britain's number-one tennis star to the semi-finals passed by almost unnoticed, buried beneath a tide of information about the dietary preferences of the Paraguayan back four. England are being hammered at cricket again. London is hot, sticky and grimy. And I am on my way to a football match.

That's why I am here, mixing my sweat with that of the commuters of London, feeling my shirt sticking to my back and my jeans creasing in an uncomfortably damp way at the backs of my knees. All this to go and watch a reserve team take on a fair-to-middling non-league side far away in the commuter belt at the height of summer. Stevenage Borough against Charlton Athletic. Here we go again. Sigh.

The 1997–98 season was a cracking one for London. Arsenal did the double. Chelsea finished fourth in the FA Carling Premiership and won the European Cup-Winners' Cup and the Coca-Cola Cup. Charlton Athletic's astonishing penalty-shoot-out victory over Sunderland at Wembley means that at the start of the 1998–99 campaign almost one third of the Premiership will hail from the capital. (Only Palace let the city down, relegated by a mile and almost going an entire season without winning at home.) Two London-based players turned out for the winning side in the World Cup final; one of them even scored a goal.

This book was originally intended to be a chronicle of the 1998–99 season in London. It didn't turn out that way. I'd set out to find whether there was a football spirit unique to the metropolis, a binding ethos that draws together fans and players from all levels and walks of life who are based in the capital.

Pretty early I concluded that there isn't such a thing. A conglomeration of various replica shirts queuing at Charing Cross McDonald's at 5.30 on a Saturday afternoon is about as close as you're likely to get to a shared London football experience. There are a number of intra-city rivalries – Arsenal and Tottenham, Chelsea and West Ham, Fulham and Brentford and so on – but no sense of London pride as such. Most fans of the capital's clubs were willing Arsenal to retain the title once their own hopes had been snuffed out, but perhaps that owed more to an anti-Manchester United bias than metropolitan loyalty.

Instead I found that London can be taken as a case study for the current state of the game as a whole, from the bright lights and razzmatazz of the FA Carling Premiership to the sweaty socks and talent-economic endeavour of Sunday football. Whilst Charlton count the cost of relegation from the Premier League as well as ruing the fact that they could sell out their stadium twice over for many fixtures, Tooting and Mitcham United find that they can barely fill their dilapidated ground some eight divisions below and so are selling up and moving into a smaller home.

As much football life as possible features here. What you won't find are detailed analyses of the plight of Crystal Palace or the rapid rise of Fulham. Whilst the two clubs' respective situations are symptomatic of what is wrong with the current game, they have been and will be chronicled by better-qualified people than I. There's probably enough material for a book on each. Plus the lengthy period of time between me completing this manuscript and it appearing on the shelves means that their situations will have changed dramatically, rendering irrelevant any half-baked, beard-stroking musings that I might have come up with. A long-simmering and irrational dislike of the Eagles also means that it's probably best if I don't urinate on their particular bonfire any more than they are doing themselves.

I followed the FA Cup, in some way, shape or form, through the 1998–99 season from the preliminary round to the final. This way I hoped to see the game at all levels. Rather than start with one team and follow that particular thread through the competition, I instead chose, just about randomly, a tie from each round in the capital.

But Arsenal's trophyless season, Charlton's relegation, Fulham's storming of the Second Division and Chelsea's gallant attempt to retain their European prize are all a long way off as I disembark at Stevenage station. Over the coming season I will meet players and football characters famous and unknown. I will even develop a tolerance of Arsenal that I never possessed before, and see Wimbledon more times than I will see my own team. I shall even develop a grudging respect for Millwall. But today I am in Stevenage.

Stevenage is a typical commuter town. It's all concentric ring roads and roundabouts linking tarmac expanses which surround low-level corrugated furniture, electrical and DIY stores. I trudge amongst the coarse, long grass that seems to grow only in these charmless places in search of the place where Newcastle United so nearly came a spectacular, whinging cropper the season before. The place where the Toon disgracefully played the Hillsborough card because they didn't fancy a trip to a modern, well-appointed and above all very safe football ground, one which puts several lower-division clubs to shame. If only Stevenage had done it. If only the linesman hadn't bottled out of indicating that Shearer's shot hadn't actually crossed the line instead of being taken in by the striker's barely credible celebration. He knew it hadn't gone in.

As I crossed another roundabout, or perhaps one I'd already crossed – they all look the same around here – I asked directions from a man who turned out to be probably the only Charlton supporter in Stevenage. A vertically challenged middle-aged man, he sported a jacket decorated with a huge check design, the sort of garment last seen in early-'70s detective shows like *Columbo* and *Charlie's Angels*, with lapels wide enough to make the traffic swerve around them as we tramped through the long grass at the roadside.

My guide took advantage of his captive audience to regale me with tales of Charlton's past, when 80,000 apparently used to watch the Addicks. How Sam Bartram used to have a good ten yards of space around him in the penalty area because everyone, defenders and opposition forwards alike, would be pounded into the turf by the big goalkeeper if they got any closer. Yes, steamroller them he would – not afraid to use his fists, neither, was Sam. Taller than the crossbar he was, and when he spread his arms they were wider than the goalposts. Hands the size of a pair of woks. I didn't have the heart nor the inclination to suggest that perhaps the passing years had distorted this estimation of the great man's abilities.

By this time we had reached Broadhall Way. My companion helpfully asked a steward where the visitors' enclosure was, to a wry smile from myself. As if a pre-season friendly between a Conference team and a reserve team would be segregated. I was startled to be shown towards a turnstile marked for the use of visitors.

So it was that I found myself in a crowd of 2,365 at an end populated by about 20 Charlton supporters. As I stood behind the goal clutching my teamsheet and trying to recognise some of the Charlton players warming up, I was hit by the two smells that indicate that the football season is back: burnt onions and liniment. Smells as comforting and homely as that of a freshly laundered pair of underpants. A little over two months had passed since that day at Wembley when 35,000 Addicks fans had roared the team on to that extraordinary play-off victory over Sunderland. The small gathering of fans lounging on the terrace with me still bore that distant half-smile that everyone who was there that day still carries.

As the teams entered the field, they were accompanied by a large red bear, clumping alongside the players like a contestant on *It's a Knockout*. This was, according to the Stevenage PA announcer (a velvet-voiced master of the *mot juste* who sounds like he should have his own late-night show on Radio Two), something called Borough Bear. Mascot madness has now crept into the non-leagues. God help us. I allowed myself a wry chuckle as I wondered what the women's team Old Fallopians (nickname The Tubes) would have as a mascot. An image came to mind, and I soon stopped chuckling. Ugh.

As the two teams divided, the Stevenage players ran towards the home end and, er, some more Stevenage players ran towards the visitors. It appeared that Charlton were wearing Stevenage's away shirts for reasons beyond the comprehension of the travelling faithful. Either Charlton hadn't checked on Stevenage's colours and had packed red shirts or, more likely, the new away kit wasn't ready and Mesh Computers weren't keen on the idea of the reserve team running out for a pre-season friendly in the old Viglen-sponsored ones. Either way, the super soaraway Premiership Addicks took the field in a yellow-and-black abomination that looked like a squashed wasps' nest.

The Stevenage side contained a few names and faces familiar from their cup exploits, though unfortunately not the singer from Supergrass who had scored Borough's goal at St James's Park. Charlton's team was a mixture of youth and reserve players, along with the surprising inclusion of out-of-favour Arsenal striker Chris Kiwomya, at The Valley on trial.

The first half was goalless and uneventful, save for a large hot-air balloon which suddenly inflated and launched itself skyward from directly behind the far goal. At half-time the frustrated crooner on the microphone tried to tempt the faithful towards the Boro shop with the promise of finding some 'really superb keyrings. I saw some today and they really are absolutely superb. Do go and buy one, they're magnificent.' Presumably the early start to the season had caught the Boro shop on the hop a little, and as a result new stock was a little scarce. This was the only time the smooth-talking devil on the mike floundered. He didn't even stumble over the name of Charlton's Nigerian central defender Emeka Ifejiagwa. What a pro.

In the second half Charlton took control and rattled in four good goals, the pick of which was an exquisite chip into the top corner by Kiwomya. As we left the ground, the small Charlton faithful nodded to each other, exchanged 'looks like we'll have strength in depth this year' comments and headed for the station. So now when the hordes of New Charlton fans in the pub start to discuss the team, I can chip in and tell them what a great goal Kevin Lisbie scored at Stevenage, and how Kemi Izzet and Leigh Hales look great prospects. I will impart this information with an air of all-seeing wisdom before turning and walking away, head held high, knowing that I know more about Charlton than they ever will. They, of course, will think that I'm a bit of a wanker.

As I waited for my connection at Stevenage station, perhaps even on the very spot where Gazza had his famous breakdown, I realised that non-stop, year-round football is all but with us. No sooner does one season finish than another is kicking off before you've had time to fill in your season-ticket application. Next season, the league campaign will commence a week earlier, in order to allow the two clubs involved in the Champions' League a bit of extra time to fit in their gruelling European schedule (even though they backed the expanded Champions' League format). The crop of monthly magazines boasting the full season review are still on the shelves as the new campaign officially kicks off, which for me it does at Brentford a few days after my Stevenage escapade.

Now the real fun starts. It's still a week away from the commencement of the pirate mercenary breakaway league otherwise known as the FA Carling Premiership, but the pubs around Griffin Park are packed with people sporting red-and-white striped shirts. For today, in the summer sunshine with temperatures soaring way into the eighties, the Nation-wide League commences. Rather than the fanfare and blaze of publicity that will herald the start of the Premiership season, the Nationwide gets little more than a grunt of acknowledgement from the armchair supporters of the nation to whom the modern game is tailored. But to the fans of Nationwide clubs, today is the real start to the season. You wouldn't think it to look at the season previews falling to the floor from every national newspaper, though – 95 per cent of the coverage is dedicated to the Premier League.

It is a sweltering day with the sun beating down from a cloudless sky. The man-made fibres sported by the Bees' fans threaten to melt and weld to their skin, and the apparent technology and research that goes into these shoddy abominations to justify the extortionate prices charged for them are shown up to be the marketing hype that they are. The shirts are uncomfortable and impractical during the summer and uncomfortable and impractical during the winter. Today you can almost hear them sizzling and crackling in the heat, and the traditional football smells of burgers and cigarette smoke are replaced by Ambre Solaire and baked sweat as some of west London's damper armpits descend upon Griffin Park.

Given that this was the hottest day of the year and that I am blessed with the sort of complexion that starts to turn pink while watching the Holiday Programme on television, perhaps standing in the uncovered Ealing Road end was not, on reflection, the best option. And there was certainly a great deal of reflection behind the goal that day, from shiny football shirts, rashly exposed sweat-sheened bellies and glossy bald heads. The aeroplanes that swoop noisily over the ground as they approach Heathrow at an altitude of a few hundred feet were put in serious danger as dazzled pilots, blinded by a sea of garish bri-nylon and greased, sunburnt beerbellies, threw their arms across their faces and screamed 'Aaaiieeeeeeee!!' as their aircraft ploughed into the M4 in a blaze of flame and burning aircraft fuel. Death by replica shirts. It will happen. You mark my words.

This being the first game of the season, the Brentford faithful were sporting the entire range of World Cup souvenirs: T-shirts, baseball caps, plastic drinks beakers – the legacy of France '98 lingered on, with its logo smeared on to anything with a space. Possibly the smuggest-looking people behind the goal were a middle-aged couple in pristine, crisp white T-shirts bearing the slightly confused legend 'Lineker's Bar, Tenerife – World Cup, France 98'. They'd obviously kept the shirts unworn for this very occasion, the show-offs.

If it wasn't for the inappropriate weather, this visit to Griffin Park would have been like a trip back to the good old days before football was groovy: standing behind the goal, singing, cardboard burgers and burnt onions, swigging warm cherryade from a tiny plastic bottle containing enough E-numbers to make feasible a couple of rounds of bingo, and Ron Noades showing himself up again.

For Ron, silver of hair and of tongue, had taken control of Brentford during the close-season after the former Chelsea defender David Webb had finally been ousted from his position as chief executive. As at Torquay, Bournemouth and Southend before, Webb's conduct as a businessman had led to the Bees' fans clamouring for his removal. Under his tutelage the Bees had gone from just missing out on a place in the First Division following defeat at Wembley in the play-off final to an ignominious relegation to the Third in the space of a season.

Enter kind Uncle Ron on his white charger.

Noades has launched the managerial careers of a number of leading gaffers: Dave Bassett, Alan Smith, Steve Coppell and, er, Attilio Lombardo to name but a few. So Brentford fans waited with baited breath to discover who their new supremo would be. Opening the programme, the horrible truth became clear. Peering out from the page titled 'From the Managers (sic) Bench' was a photograph of the man himself. Ron was the manager, the boss, the gaffer, whatever you will. The picture showed Ron actually smiling, although it was obviously an unfamiliar experience as he wasn't doing it very well. It looked like the photographer had inserted his forefingers into the corners of Ron's mouth, hoisted them upwards in the direction of his cheeks, instructed the new boss to 'hold it right there' and rushed back behind the camera to capture the moment for posterity before the lower half of Noades's face came crashing down again like glaciers melting in the polar sunshine.

His column made fascinating reading, despite turning out to be incorrectly titled. Ron revealed that he wouldn't be watching games from the touchline, nor would he seek to become a 'tracksuit manager' (isn't that job down to the kit man?). He continued, ominously, 'I have had my time of raising funds for other managers to spend on players and then taking responsibility for their actions. It will now be totally down to me . . . and I won't have to seek a vote of confidence! And before long I shall rule the world, ahahahahahahaaaa!' Okay, I made the last sentence up, but a chairman appointing himself as manager is definitely a novelty, and one that leaves the shy, retiring Noades wide open to derision. A few chairmen have tried it surreptitiously, subtly interfering with team affairs, but, fair play to Ron, he's been the first to do it openly.

At that point the unforgiving sun started to burn through the programme and Ron's face began to blacken and combust like the map in the opening titles of *Bonanza*. Phew, it was a scorcher.

The teams took the field as the tannoy honked inaudibly somewhere at the back of the terrace. Brentford looked focused, fit and prepared for the job in hand. Mansfield looked thoroughly dejected, stoop-shouldered and miserable. The Stags are in a bit of a financial mess, with the PFA imposing a transfer embargo upon them after the players were not paid for two months towards the end of the 1997–98 season. Meanwhile, the club is about to embark upon a £5 million redevelop-ment of their Field Mill ground, a venture which may bode well for the future but which hasn't pleased the Field Mill faithful. The sale of leading scorer Steve Whitehall to troubled Oldham Athletic for just £50,000 didn't increase the confidence of the fans in the team's immediate future and probably explains why the away end was so sparsely populated. The Stags looked like a beaten team before they'd even started the season.

They're a funny team, Mansfield. One of those clubs that's just, well, there. They've had no glorious yet unsuccessful seasons in the top flight, no famous cup runs to recall on *Football Focus*. In 1997–98 they finished a spectacularly average 12th in Division Three and went out of both domestic cups at the first attempt. Desperate to find something remotely interesting about the Stags, I scanned an article in the programme with the irresistible title of 'Mansfield Through the Ages'. It turned out that the Stags' glory season was one Second Division campaign in 1978 which ended in relegation. They did win the Freight Rover Trophy in 1987, mind, which gave the long-suffering fans a day out at Wembley, but hasn't everybody been to Wembley now?

Brentford fielded five new faces, with fans discussing the merits of 'that new lad from Slough' and 'the geezer we signed from Hampton'. The true fans made it plain that they'd been to all the friendlies by loudly exhorting the new boys to greater effort using their first names – with the obligatory addendum of -y or -o, of course. The side also included former Portsmouth and Villa midfielder Warren Aspinall, who looked like the oldest man still to be playing football, his shiny cranium sparsely covered by cropped grey hair. It was a little disconcerting to find out that he was barely 30. Why do footballers seem to age much faster than the rest of humanity?

The visitors paraded the usual crop of lower-division journeymen struggling to pay the mortgage and lurching from yearly contract to yearly contract. In Iyesden Christie they possessed the obligatory lower-division hothead. Usually some way under the six-foot mark, these players are blessed with no little ability but this is obscured by displays of petulance, shirt-pulling, diving, scrapping and blatant attempts to con the referee. The sort of player described in programmes as 'competitive'. They've usually come on a free from a big club and still have their best years ahead of them. Christie was signed from Coventry City, not usually known for tolerating the tantrums and general flouncing about that he displayed with such expertise.

Mansfield surprised themselves by creating the first chance of the game, a sweetly struck free-kick from 25 yards from Tony Lormor which Brentford keeper Jason Pearcey did well to reach but allowed to squirm through his hands and go round for a corner. Christie himself could have given the visitors the lead shortly afterwards when Aspinall stood on the ball in the penalty area, but his stinging close-range effort was well smothered by Pearcey. Christie reacted by jumping up and down on the spot like a spoilt child who had just dropped his ice lolly on to the pavement.

Instead of being buoyed by this bright opening, the visitors still seemed content to plod around the midfield with the kind of expressions that the artist who created Droopy the cartoon dog would have dismissed as being too miserable. It was no surprise when Brentford took the lead after half an hour, veteran goalkeeper Steve Cherry spilling a shot from Martin Rowland, another of the Bees' non-league discoveries, for Kevin Rapley to stab the ball into the net in front of the visiting fans. So disconsolate were they that you could almost see the little black cloud that hovered over their heads.

Still the sun beat relentlessly down. If this game had been a cartoon, my tongue would have been hanging out with a cactus growing out of it. I could tell that my nose, not exactly a minor feature of my face, was gently frying. At least I'd have no trouble crossing the road on the way home, as the traffic would stop and wait for my proboscis to turn green.

Eventually the Brentford team strode confidently on to the pitch whilst the Mansfield players mooched sullenly out of the tunnel for the second half. You could almost see the hands pushing them out of the door. The arrival of the ancient Mansfield goalkeeper Steve Cherry at the Ealing Road end was the cue for much hilarity due to the custodian's girth. Much of it didn't pass beyond the imaginative 'You fat bastard!', but one comment was an early contender for the surrealist-of-the-season award. Once the number of expletives that could be prefixed with the word 'fat' had been exhausted, an educated voice suddenly broke the lull with the words 'Two pounds of Pilsbury dough, goalkeeper!'. Now I don't have any idea what that means, although its reference to weights and measures implies a degree of lampooning Cherry's waistline. However, the comment was greeted by the fan's comrades with a confused silence. It was obviously something he'd been saving, as he had carefully waited for his moment and let rip with exquisite timing. Unfortunately his material was just too bizarre. Even Steve Cherry, who must have had every fat joke in the repertoire hurled at him from behind the goal-mouths of England, looked temporarily befuddled.

Cherry didn't help his cause by injuring himself in a collision with Brentford's Lloyd Owusu in the opening minutes of the half. The knock to his thigh meant that he had to hand over goal-kicking responsibilities to his defenders, which of course made him a poof. A fat poof at that. Not only that, but he was an old fat poof into the bargain. The Brentford fans thought that all their Christmases had come at once. The Pilsbury dough man kept quiet.

With a few minutes remaining, as fans in exposed areas of the ground began to spontaneously combust, I realised the heat had finally got to me when I had a sudden vision of Jesus Christ wearing full Brentford kit. He was standing at the side of the pitch spreading his arms skyward, his hair flowing down his back. I grabbed the arm of my companion, pointing and gibbering, 'Can you see it? It's Him! He is risen! And He's in full Brentford kit!'

'Oh, that's Darren Freeman. They've just signed him from Fulham. He must be coming on,' came the disappointingly secular reply. Ah well, I guess I'll have to stick to football for spiritual fulfilment.

Not entirely convinced that this wasn't the Second Coming, I watched the burly substitute enter the fray. Almost immediately a long ball was sprayed out to the right and Freeman was after it, hurtling along like an escaped hog. After one touch to control the ball, he turned and clumped a humdinger of a shot past Cherry at the near post for the third goal. No, it definitely wasn't Jesus. He'd have hit it first time.

It was a brilliant goal. The crowd roared their approval and Freeman sprinted towards the bench, gesticulating extravagantly along the lines of 'That'll teach you to put me on the bench, you clueless bastards'. He spent the final minutes of the game chasing the ball around the field like a man possessed, instantly winning over the Brentford fans on his debut.

Finally the whistle went for the end of the game. 'Going up!' sang the Bees' faithful with tongues firmly planted in cheeks. But, as it turned out, they were absolutely right. Those of us who sniggered upon hearing that Ron was dabbling in management and rubbed our hands with glee at the prospect of his inevitable failure were forced grudgingly to concede that his dastardly plan had got off to a good start. Bah.

As we left the ground, crawling on our bellies across the concrete in search of respite from the relentless sun, it was looking good for Brentford. 'It's going to be a long, hard season for Mansfield,' I croaked knowledgeably between cracked lips. 'I reckon they'll go down to the Conference this year.' Mansfield, of course, narrowly missed out on the play-offs having been in the top six for most of the season.

And so the London season commenced. Within these pages you won't find many earth-shattering theories as to how the game should be saved. Rose-tinted nostalgia and a fiercely backward sense of traditionalism is more my cup of cocoa. Go back through history and you'll probably find my ancestors smashing agricultural machinery and arguing against progress beyond the abacus. But if all has gone to plan I will have unearthed people and issues that give hope for the future of the game. I will have shown that amongst the glitz and razzmatazz engendered by those new to the game and hoping to make a few quid, there is still a sense of what made football great to start with. What that is is hard to define, but I think most of us have a good idea. This book is written in the hope that football won't become just another branch of an already saturated leisure industry, totally abandoning the uniqueness of a pastime that helped to make it special to those of us who hold the game dear.

1,080 Minutes from Wembley

Leyton Pennant v. Wembley, FA Cup Preliminary Round

'We look ahead to today's game with the realisation that we are only 1,080 minutes from Wembley,' begin the programme notes for the FA Cup preliminary-round tie at Wadham Lodge between Ryman League First Division clubs Leyton Pennant and Wembley. We've just crept into September and the greatest knockout competition in the world is under way again. Across the country 172 clubs from the lower to middling reaches of the non-league pyramid are lining up hoping for a victory that will reward them with a money-spinning tie with a Ryman, Dr Marten's or Unibond League Premier Division side. Half those teams' dreams of cup glory will end today or in a replay later in the week, and so it will be that Atherton Collieries, Shotton Comrades, Stourport Swifts, Cowes Sports, Bemerton Heath Harlequins and many others will find themselves free to concentrate on the league after today's games.

And so will struggling Wembley. The team which shares its locality with the national stadium has suffered a poor start to the season in Division One of the Ryman League, three levels below the Third Division of the Football League. The league table shows Wembley occupying bottom place in the table with four defeats from four games and a miserly one goal to their name. Last season, the Vale Farm club finished sixth from bottom and lost both games against Pennant. Leyton Pennant, thanks to a 1–1 draw with Chertsey Town earlier in the week, lie three places above them with a draw and three defeats. Worthing and Berkhamsted Town separate the two teams in the table.

'FA Cup – All Pay' reads the marker-penned notice – now ink-streaked, following the rain that has fallen all morning – pinned to the turnstiles at Wadham Lodge, a well-appointed sports ground in Walthamstow. Within the complex, where several other games take place this afternoon, is the enclosed arena that is home to Leyton Pennant, the club which has emerged from the amalgamation in 1995 of Leyton (formerly Leyton-Wingate, and before that just Leyton again) and Walthamstow Pennant, the original occupants of the ground.

East London appears to have a remarkable capacity for eating up football clubs. Leyton Pennant are now an amalgamation of Leyton, Wingate, Leyton-Wingate and Walthamstow Pennant. Take another example. Many years ago, Leytonstone and Ilford were major forces in the amateur game. In the mid-'80s they joined forces to become Leytonstone-Ilford. A couple of years later, the famous Walthamstow Avenue joined the fold but, the name Leytonstone-Ilford-Walthamstow Avenue being a touch unwieldy, the new outfit became Redbridge Forest. A couple of years later, however, Redbridge Forest moved in with Dagenham to become the current Dagenham and Redbridge. A total of five old clubs in one. I suppose the next logical step is Leyton and Dagenham Pennant. Or Pennant and Redbridge. Or Leytonbridge Dagenpennant. Or something.

'We're actually one of the oldest clubs in the country,' says Andy Perkins, Leyton Pennant's honorary secretary. 'The original Leyton club was formed in 1868, and that's where our roots lie.'

The club has an illustrious history. At the turn of the century, Leyton virtually owned the Essex Senior Cup, and by the 1920s they were one of the country's leading amateur clubs. They won the London League on three occasions and the FA Amateur Cup in 1927 after defeating Barking in a thrilling final at Millwall. They retained the trophy by beating a team of unemployed miners, Cockfield, at Middlesbrough, and reached the final again in 1929, only to lose to Ilford at Highbury. The following season, Leyton's captain, John Preston, was selected for the England team that beat Scotland that year.

At the time, the club was playing on the site of the current Leyton Orient ground. 'Yes, our first real home was at Brisbane Road,' sighs Perkins, a quietly spoken schoolteacher from nearby Wanstead. 'I've got pictures at home of people building the place. Then there was some skulduggery just before the last war, we were kicked out and the Orient moved in. Whenever I see Brisbane Road, I think to myself, that's our ground, that is.'

Neighbours Walthamstow Avenue temporarily accommodated the nomadic Leyton, before they finally settled at a ground behind the Hare and Hounds pub on Lea Bridge Road. In 1952 the club ploughed through all the qualifying rounds of the Amateur Cup to reach the final at Wembley. They played 12 games in all, as well as one tie with Eton Manor which was abandoned at half-time. In the final, Leyton went down to Walthamstow Avenue and a goal two minutes from the end of extra time in front of a near-capacity crowd. Ironically, the Lilywhites' first opponents in that campaign were Wembley. It's highly unlikely that this season will produce a Wembley to Wembley sequence for the club.

Wadham Lodge is a smart, modern ground, more than suited to Pennant's status. A neat 200-seater stand straddles the halfway line and there's covered accommodation for 600 behind the goal, with shallow terracing all the way around the pitch. A large clubhouse overlooks the pitch from behind the stand. There is considerable scope for growth, and Pennant are obviously ambitious. 'We've applied for a Lottery grant so that we can put cover behind the far goal and extend the stand,' says Perkins. 'That way we can get an A grading from the League.'

Notwithstanding the modern appearance of the ground, Leyton Pennant are proud of their history. Dominating the club shop, in which you can buy club scarves, replica shirts (the 'fashion statement of the year', according to the programme) and, of course, pennants, is the old honours board from Lea Bridge Road. Looking rather unwieldy affixed to the wall of a portakabin, the huge dark-oak board reveals in fading gold lettering the former club's illustrious honours and amateur inter-nationals. Beneath the board, oblivious middle-aged men with dandruff and carrier bags rummage through the boxes looking for that elusive Abingdon Town v. Ware programme from the 1985–86 season. You know, the one with the misprint on page six.

The attendance is disappointing. Barely a hundred spectators are in the ground as the kick-off approaches, and I ask Andy Perkins whether the fact that Leyton Orient are entertaining Carlisle United just down the road has affected the gate.

'Not really,' he sniffs, looking wistfully around the near-empty ground. 'We like to think that Orient being at home affects the gates, but to be honest there's only about seven or eight guys that I'd recognise as only coming to see us when the O's are away. I don't think it really affects us at all.'

As we walk behind the goal, the Pennant players are warming up, taking pot shots at the empty net. The three players lining up have managed to despatch all the training balls over the goal and out of the ground, a profligacy of finishing that doesn't bode well for the rest of the afternoon. As they wait sheepishly for their return, a voice wafts from the car park behind. 'Why don't you bloody learn to shoot properly?' bawls an irritated car-park attendant. The players collect the balls as they are launched back into the ground and troop back to the dressing-room for the final pep talk. The PA announcer reads the teams out very slowly. So

23

slowly, in fact, that by the time he's halfway through the Wembley line-up it appears that he's actually dozed off.

Suddenly the Wembley team in their all-yellow strip run out of the dressing-room and on to the pitch, jumping, stretching and doing that peculiar sideways run that players do. A few seconds later the referee summons them back to the tunnel because, of course, in the FA Cup the teams have to emerge on to the pitch together. In one of their more decisive moments, the Association decreed that the tradition of the away team running out first to be roundly booed followed by the home side to rapturous cheers should stop. The two teams must come out of the tunnel neck and neck. Now this is fine at Premiership grounds, where the tunnels are wide enough for Vanessa Feltz and Luciano Pavarotti to emerge hand in hand and side by side, but at this level most clubs have little more than your average doorway. The day will surely come when kick-off is delayed because the players are wedged in the tunnel. So at the second attempt, the two sides emerge awkwardly on to the hallowed turf of Wadham Lodge to do battle in the FA Cup preliminary round.

'The sponsors wanted us to take a photo of the team in the new kit, but the manager won't have it. He says it's superstition,' says Perkins. 'We asked him to do it at the first game of the season against Bognor, but he wouldn't have it for the same reason: he reckons it's bad luck. We lost 2–1 that day.'

The Wembley away following – two blokes with severe crew cuts, enormous mutton-chop sideburns, check shirts and Harrington jackets – troop towards the goal occupied by Pennant's keeper Clark Wells and affix their flag of St George emblazoned with the legend 'Wembley FC' to the barrier. Throughout the game they keep up a constant stream of encouragement. The roar they both produce when Wembley win their first corner would put some Premiership grounds to shame.

Pennant open brightly and appear to have taken the lead when their portly striker Billy Cove lashes one in, only for the goal to be disallowed for offside. Wembley immediately build an attack at the other end, but the pass goes astray. 'You fucking idiot!' screams the potential recipient to his errant team-mate, encouragingly.

Wembley look the better side, and up front for Leyton Billy Cove is having a nightmare. His first touch lets him down every time, and when a team-mate threads an impressive lobbed pass between two defenders, Cove misreads the flight and the ball hits him square on his well-upholstered backside before bouncing to safety. His head drops, and he fails to reappear for the second half. So lacklustre has their first-half performance been that manager Kevin Moran (no, not that one) keeps his side on the pitch during the interval for extra training. This plan appears to backfire as ten minutes after the interval Pennant's Billy Read, one of the more impressive players on the field, tries to play his way out of danger, slips, and releases the ball to Wembley's Jesse Hall. Hall takes the ball around Wells to give the visitors a deserved lead. The cheer that goes up reveals a strong Wembley presence in the crowd of around 120, and the two blokes behind the goal go berserk, leaping around the terraces looking from a distance like they're being attacked by a swarm of killer bees.

Ten minutes later, Mitchell Evans capitalises on another poor clearance, Pennant are back on level terms and they are finally beginning to gain the upper hand. Despite the sending-off of stocky centre-half John-Paul Kent, Che Stadart emphatically finishes a cross from right-back Cyril Baffour to give the home side the lead with a quarter of an hour remaining. Wembley press for an equaliser as the minutes tick away, and tempers become frayed. Corners are wasted, arguments break out between team-mates, substitutes are thrown on to no avail and the home side hangs on to chalk up their first win of the season. Their reward is a trip to Ware, from the Ryman League Third Division, two divisions below their own.

'Obviously we'd have liked Aldershot in the next round,' says Andy Perkins. Aldershot Town, born from the ashes of the old Aldershot club, are the Holy Grail for non-league clubs (and their bank managers) in the south. Last season Leyton Pennant's trip to Hampshire resulted in an 8–1 caning in front of over 2,000, but the league game at Wadham Lodge drew slightly less. 'We were supposed to play them on a Saturday, and expected a crowd of about 2,000. But they had to play a Hampshire Senior Cup game at Newport, Isle of Wight, that day instead. Because you can't get ferries from the Isle of Wight late at night, Newport have to play games on a Saturday afternoon. So we played Aldershot on the Tuesday, it pissed down and only 400 people turned up.'

At least the trip to Ware gives Pennant hope of a straightforward progression to the second qualifying round. It's not to be, though, and Leyton Pennant's hopes of a financial windfall from the FA Cup will be ended by a 2–0 defeat at the hands of the lowly Hertfordshire side.

Today has been a good day for Pennant, though, their first FA Cup win for three years. It seems the team responded to Charlie Ward's exhortations in the programme. 'What has happened to the fighting spirit?' he asked of the club's unimpressive start to the season. 'We have seen the ability of the players in the side, we have been tearing teams apart already this year but only in short spells, and we now need to see this converted over the whole game. In other words, will the real Leyton Pennant present themselves at 3 p.m. today and show us how it can be done.'

But the Wembley trail ends for Wembley at the first hurdle. The FA Cup has begun, and 86 clubs are out already. Bacup Borough of the North-West Counties League were the first to go through: their preliminary-round opponents Blackpool Wren Rovers pulled out of the competition after the draw had been made. Leyton Pennant's Wembley dreams are to last less than two weeks. Having battered a side from the division above, ten days later they cave in to a club two divisions below. Funny old game, eh ?

Pride Not Prejudice

Ken Chapman in the Lions' Den

The name Millwall doesn't immediately conjure up the image of a progressive, community-minded football club. Deserved or not, a section of the Bermondsey club's followers have a reputation for violence, intimidation and racism. Many football fans still shudder when recalling trips to The Den down dark, warren-like backstreets ideal for ambushes, before enduring the taunts and threats of certain sections of the home support inside the ground. The away end at Cold Blow Lane was a pen behind a floodlight where you were hemmed in with a restricted view and subjected to the taunts and sharpened coins of south London's finest sons.

Just before they left The Den in 1993, I recall standing amongst the Millwall supporters behind the goal at a match against Derby County and being stunned at the casual racism being bandied around. This wasn't just chanting, but conversational observations about 'fucking niggers' and so on. It was racism with a smile and a chuckle, with no sense that what they were saying was in any way wrong or even contentious. I'd always given Millwall the benefit of the doubt (after all, two of my cousins had been first-team regulars at The Den, so I'd often been to watch them), but after that day I realised how deep-seated the malaise appeared to be. During the late '80s and early '90s the club seemed to deny that there was a problem, despite the startling evidence to the contrary.

Thankfully, a visit to Millwall today is a different proposition. They now play at the New Den in south Bermondsey, a neat if bland stadium that has none of the intimidating characteristics that made its predecessor so notorious. The walk to the ground is still not particularly pleasant: the station is high and unprotected on a windswept embankment, and British National Party stickers adorn the lampposts on the long walkway to ground level. Most have been at least partially scratched off. You arrive at the ground by passing under a low, damp railway arch but emerge into a clean, well-designed ground. The blue paint may be fading and the roof supports rusting, but it's still a much nicer place to visit than Cold Blow Lane.

Millwall have made great strides towards cleaning up their image. They have set up community-based initiatives, and even offered match-day crèche facilities in an attempt to haul themselves into the modern age. Their Community Sports Scheme, established as long ago as 1985, offers special-needs coaching, teacher training, after-school clubs, holiday courses, a sports-scholarship scheme and even a truancy project. And, gratifyingly, they have set about addressing the problem of racism with firm commitment.

In 1994, Millwall set up an Anti-Racism Committee with the help of the police, Lewisham Council, Southwark Council, the Let's Kick Racism Out Of Football campaign and local community groups. Ken Chapman, a retired police officer, holds down what some might regard as the two hardest jobs in football: Anti-Racism Committee Co-ordinator and Security Adviser to Millwall FC.

Chapman, a bespectacled, grey-haired Lancastrian who is a self-confessed Preston North End supporter ('when Preston visit The Den I sit on the halfway line'), is a busy man. He has to cancel our first meeting as it falls just after Millwall's match at Manchester City where the London club's fans were involved in skirmishes with the opposition and were on the receiving end of some harsh treatment by the Manchester Police. 'I'm tied up with taking photographs of bruises and taking statements from people,' he explains apologetically. Instead he invites me to Millwall's Auto-Windscreens Shield tie with Gillingham the following week.

Millwall slash seat prices for the fixture to just five pounds, hence a crowd of over 11,000 turns out for what otherwise might have been a sparsely attended match. I arrive early and sit talking to Chapman in the Millwall press lounge. In the corner, the club are launching a museum. It's a bit low on exhibits at the moment (well, there's a couple of shirt-wearing mannequins) but the walls are adorned with cartoons and press cuttings going way back through the club's history.

Also on the walls, blu-tacked rather than framed, are some of the posters produced by a fan to support Chapman's anti-racist initiative. 'Lions have pride, not prejudice,' reads the slogan.

Chapman attacks racism at the club with forthright assertiveness. In every home programme there is a message which reads: 'Our concern is that the passion and emotion created at football matches does not exceed the boundaries of reasonable behaviour. Passionate support does not need indecent, obscene or racist comments or actions. Respect each other, respect all fans. Anyone who is genuinely offended by the behaviour of others in their vicinity should in the first instance report the matter to the nearest steward or police officer. Alternatively they may do so in writing or by phone to Colin Sayer or Kenneth Chapman at the club. Help us to help our club.'

It is messages such as these, as well as more assertive stewarding and a greater awareness by the police of the problem of racism at football grounds, that have led to a notable decrease in racist chanting at matches. But it is also the actions of the supporters themselves which have helped.

There is a definite cultural shift happening inside football grounds. No longer are they the preserve of young, white men they once were. A growing number of supporters from ethnic minorities are present at grounds today, perhaps due to the proliferation of black, or more specifically Afro-Caribbean, players that has become the norm in the modern game. The days when Laurie Cunningham, John Chiedozie and suchlike were a rarity, even a novelty, are long gone.

Chapman himself wrote an article for the Millwall v. Walsall programme, a game which was used by the club as an anti-racism focus day, which detailed the contribution Millwall's black players have made to the club over the years, from Frank Peterson and John Fashanu to Bobby Bowry in the current line-up.

A number of clubs have actively campaigned against racism in their stadia, setting up initiatives and producing literature in an effort to stamp it out. South-east London has been a particular hotspot, especially as the British National Party is based there and the racist murders of victims such as Stephen Lawrence in Eltham and Rolan Adams in Thamesmead have occurred there in recent years.

It was the acknowledgement that south London had a problem which led to the south London initiative, undertaken by Charlton, Crystal Palace and Millwall together with local councils and Football In The Community schemes. A specially produced eight-page tabloid news-paper was distributed to 200,000 homes in the region, carrying the message that it is the colour of the shirt that counts. The clubs co-ordinated anti-racist focus days, along the lines of Charlton's long-running 'Red, White and Black' days, where thousands of tickets were distributed to local ethnic-minority community groups.

Outside London, Northampton Town have embarked upon a long-term anti-racist campaign, giving away tickets to ethnic-minority

organisations and encouraging the town's sizeable Bangladeshi population to take up the game. The club was the first to introduce an Equal
Opportunity policy for its staff. Exeter City, Leyton Orient, West Brom-
wich Albion and Preston North End are among clubs commended by the
Kick It Out campaign for their anti-racist activities.

Since Chapman's arrival at The Den, where his brief is supposed to be
for two days per week but rarely works out that way, and the establishment of the anti-racist initiative, there has been a marked decrease in
overt racism at Millwall. 'We have had a number of successful convic-
tions,' says Chapman, who with his spectacles, grey hair, shirt and tie
looks more like a recently retired bank clerk than someone taking up the
cudgels against racist thugs. 'We have 31 people banned from the ground
at the moment for racist activity. The bans are indefinite and are reviewed
at the end of each season. But the frustrating thing is that we can only
ban them from the New Den. The courts will not enforce exclusion
orders. This means that despite their being banned from Millwall home
matches, these characters are free to travel to away games. There are two
notorious supporters currently excluded from the ground who can be
seen sitting in the pub at the end of the road from the ground before and
after every home game. It is annoying because the courts could and
should use the powers that are available to them.'

Chapman's frustration also appears to stem from the feeling that his
hands are tied a little. He feels that the Millwall initiative isn't receiving
all the help it could. 'We've taken a positive stance to rid Millwall and
football of racism, but this committee has taken things just about as far
as it can,' he says. 'We're only voluntary, and we need to formalise some
kind of ad-hoc committee, a stand-alone company which can draw
money into the project. We also need to forge closer ties with Lewisham
and Southwark Councils whereby we can involve more black and ethnic-
minority youngsters, foster relationships through a good community
scheme in schools but then follow it up when the kids have left school.
As most people know, Millwall has been in the financial doldrums over
recent seasons, and although that situation has been reversed, there still
isn't much money around. Twenty-four staff lost their jobs when we had
the administrators in, whilst everyone who remained had a 10 per cent
wage cut. But with the new chairman here, things are definitely looking
much more positive.'

Millwall chairman Theo Paphitis is one of very few club chairmen to
hail from an ethnic-minority background. The chairman of Rymans, the
stationery chain, and the Contessa and La Senza lingerie stores, Paphitis has
been at the front of Millwall's campaigns against racism at the New Den.

'The chairman is trying to build a lean, successful club here,' explains Chapman. 'He's very interested in the youth set-up here. We have an excellent youth team which is doing magnificently well in this season's FA Youth Cup, and a number of these promising players coming up through the youth ranks are drawn from local ethnic-minority communities, which is a really encouraging sign.'

The club have also built strong links with the Khalsa Football Federation, a Midlands-based organisation dedicated to the promotion of Asian players within football. Over a decade old, the Khalsa Federation provides a showcase of Asian talent. As well as Millwall, Khalsa has played a youth fixture against Manchester City.

Despite all the progress made by black players over recent years, there has remained a notable lack of Asians coming through the ranks. Old-guard administrations have dismissed this as a 'cultural' thing – Asian kids are more interested in chess and hockey – whilst one respected and well-known English coach memorably remarked that Asians would never make it in football because they have to kneel down and face Mecca every five minutes.

At the time of writing there are no Asians playing first-team professional football in England, despite the fact that at grass-roots level the participation is startlingly high (the Guru Nanak club, based in Gravesend, Kent, have over 100 players at various age levels). It's a curious situation, one which could be explained away as a combination of clubs' prejudice and the suspicions of Asian parents about institutions who have traditionally ignored their very presence. There are a couple of young players on the books of Premiership clubs, Amrit Sidhu at Derby County and Harpal Singh of Leeds United, but given the amount of football played by young Asians in Britain, it does seem strange that none have progressed through the ranks to professional football.

Millwall's involvement with the Khalsa Federation is a direct result of Paphitis's stewardship: some 75 per cent of employees at his company headquarters are Asian, and many play football under the Khalsa umbrella. In 1998 the Lions played a pre-season friendly against a Khalsa representative side preceded by a schoolboy match between the two sides.

'It was a very successful day,' says Chapman. 'We had over 3,000 Asians in the ground, which would have been unthinkable not too many years ago. Millwall could only field what was essentially a reserve team because the first team had played at Wigan the day before, but the standard of football was excellent. In fact, so good was the standard that Millwall signed the Khalsa Under-14 goalkeeper on associate schoolboy forms after the game.'

The day was deemed such a success that it was repeated at the start of the 1999–2000 season and may become an annual event. 'We're certainly here for the long haul,' says Chapman. 'We want to ensure a safe and friendly environment for anyone coming to Millwall by taking action against anyone who seeks to drag down the name of the club and of football in general.

'To do this we have to become heavily involved in the local community. The area around the stadium fits in with the Millwall reputation: it's run-down, not very well lit, daubed with graffiti. But despite all that we've managed to create an atmosphere where people feel safe within the ground. After all, in the London Borough of Lewisham, ethnic minorities account for 25 per cent of the population, whilst in this ward, where we're sitting, it's as high as 72 per cent. That proportion is nowhere near represented in the stands here, so we've got to work to get the local community on our side, to say, look, it is safe to come and watch football here.

'We need to build on that now, and having a successful team on the field certainly helps. We have three black regular first-team players and another half-dozen or so who play in the reserves. There's actually a white minority in the Under-17 and Under-19 teams. Change isn't going to happen overnight, no one's under any illusions there, but we do have some good role models coming through.'

As Millwall progressed to the next round of the Auto-Windscreens Shield thanks to an extra-time 'golden goal', their midfield was marshalled by Bobby Bowry, a combative, committed player in the true Millwall mould. Bowry differs from other Den favourites like Harry Cripps and Terry Hurlock only in the fact that he's black. They don't care for fancy-dans at The Den: even players like Teddy Sheringham, who scored hatfuls of goals for the Lions before embarking on a career which culminated in his scoring in the European Cup final, aren't held in particularly high regard compared to the real battlers.

Against Gillingham that night, Bowry ran the game from the midfield, winning the ball on countless occasions with steely determination, countering the mythical surmisal of a certain white-haired former chairman of a nearby club that you need good hard white players to see you through the winter.

'We've got a young player in the first team called Tim Cahill, who's from an aboriginal background,' says Chapman, 'and he's absolutely brilliant at talking to people about racial issues. The players here are generally very co-operative but I know some of them don't find it easy. Not enough players get involved – not necessarily through laziness. I think a lot of young black players are told not to become too involved in the political business of racism in football; they're warned it could be a hindrance to their careers, that it could stand in the way of future transfers and so on.'

With such effective role models, Chapman has detected a shift in the attitude of supporters who are now prepared to blow the whistle on racists in the Den crowd.

'People are now alerting us to racist incidents within the ground, so we can tackle the perpetrators. Also there's been a definite increase in fans shouting down the racists – when a fellow supporter pulls them up, they tend to take more notice. We've had six people convicted of racial abuse here as a result, which is a criminal offence.'

Chapman spends most games holed up in the police control room, scanning the crowd for signs of potential trouble. He doesn't say it in so many words, but he hints that as well as CCTV cameras, the Den may be equipped with audio facilities enabling the control box to hear racist abuse.

'Racism invariably seems to happen at times of confrontation,' he says, 'like when a black opposition player fouls a Millwall lad. That can sometimes trigger racist remarks. By training cameras on potential hotspots, we then have video evidence of racist abuse and can arrest the people responsible at the next game. That's also the reason why we have that notice in the programme: it can be hard for a supporter to point out a troublemaker at the game for fear of reprisals. If they write to me or phone me then we can pick the perpetrator up at the next match.

'We're working to create a climate where racism is just totally unacceptable. I don't think you'll ever eradicate racism altogether – after all, hooliganism of one form or another has been around since football began – but what we can do is make the ground safe for people to enter, for people from ethnic minorities to enter with peace of mind because they know that racism won't be tolerated at Millwall.'

Millwall are building an effective community scheme which goes beyond the anti-racism initiative to take in the wider picture, as Chapman elaborates. 'Football isn't a cheap activity these days. This particular ward is one of the ten poorest in London: we have high unemployment, poor housing conditions and a large percentage of local residents on some kind of state benefit. Obviously the people in this locality can't afford to shell out ten or twenty quid each to watch a football match.

'But that doesn't stop us going into the community to build positive links, to make the club an important part of the community in which it sits. We are dealing with kids who have been expelled from school, kids who can't read who receive two hours of reading classes and two hours' football coaching a week. Football has a responsibility to those sections of society who invest their money and time into following the game, and we seek to meet that responsibility head on.'

A few weeks later Millwall played Walsall at the New Den in an anti-racism focus event surrounding their Nationwide League Division Two fixture. Everyone entering the stadium was given a sticker bearing the 'Kick Out Racism' message, whilst anti-racist banners were paraded on the pitch and held up by both teams for photographs. A steel band played outside the ground and, perhaps most importantly, 1,300 tickets were distributed to local ethnic-minority groups. Although the first comment I heard after the kick-off was 'You useless Irish cunt', it was gratifying to discover that the throwaway racism I had experienced five years earlier seemed to have vanished. In fact, the perpetrator of that particular piece of Anglo-Irish relations then went on to sing Manchester United songs including a paean to United's famous Irishman: 'There's only one Keano'. Indeed, Ken Chapman, sitting in the press box as a Clubcall summariser, was called upon only once during the 90 minutes: to protect a female journalist from being unimaginatively chatted up by an amorous Millwall fan (now there's a concept to have you waking up screaming in the middle of the night) sitting in the seat adjacent to her.

Later in the season, Millwall advanced on Wembley for the Auto-Windscreens Shield final against Wigan Athletic. For any club, reaching Wembley is the ideal opportunity to go into marketing overdrive, with the full range of scarves, hats, flags and leisurewear being wheeled out with the Wembley name emblazoned somewhere. Millwall were one of the few clubs left in the country not to have appeared at Wembley in a peacetime cup or play-off final and did not hesitate to leap on to the merchandise bandwagon. However, Chapman and his colleagues also managed to use the Lions' Wembley jaunt to put across their anti-racist message. The team walked out on to the Wembley turf in training tops bearing the 'Kick Out Racism' slogan, whilst the club also used a supplement in the local press the week before the final as an anti-racist vehicle. The 'Kick It Out' logo appeared on every page of the Lions at Wembley section, and it was revealed that Millwall were taking 200 local schoolchildren to Wembley as guests of the club.

The match, transmitted live on Sky, proved to be a disappointment for the Bermondsey club, who lost to a controversial late goal. The club's old image also reared its ugly head as a section of Millwall fans chanted during the minute's silence commemorating the tenth anniversary of the

Hillsborough disaster. Not surprisingly, it was this angle that the press picked up on rather than the excellent work of Chapman, Paphitis and their cohorts.

The fight against racism is important to Ken Chapman. As a high-profile figure at the club (he often receives hate mail addressed to 'nigger-lover Ken Chapman'), he could make himself a target for far-right groups. The racial tinderbox of south-east London has come under intense scrutiny in recent years, not least due to the Stephen Lawrence case, and Chapman and Millwall are making a valuable contribution to the fight to kick racism out of football.

Chapman is not naïve enough to think that racism will be eradicated, nor will its defeat happen overnight, but he and his colleagues on the anti-racism committee have made a valuable and impressive start. At last Millwall have admitted they have a problem. For too long the old administration chose to turn the other cheek, pretending that there wasn't a problem. The arrival of Theo Paphitis has heralded a new dawn at the New Den. Millwall are arguably the only London club in what could be described as an inner-city area, and they are making great progress in going out into that community and winning over the populace. They took 45,000 people to Wembley, but only one tenth of that number attended the home league fixture against Colchester United the week before. There's still a long way to go, but the potential is obviously there. If a few more of that 45,000 can be persuaded that the New Den is a safe place to be, then perhaps there will be a few more black faces in the crowd in the future.

'We're here for the long term,' says Chapman, 'and we're already making headway. If we can put a successful team together and lift the local population, then with a professional, positive attitude we will succeed. All Millwall supporters want their players to go to heaven, just so long as they die in a blue shirt.'

The Devil Went Down to Clapton

Clapton v. Tilbury, FA Cup First Qualifying Round

If visiting Leyton Pennant is like calling on an energetic nephew, then a trip to the Old Spotted Dog ground in Forest Gate, the home of Clapton Football Club, is like visiting an elderly aunt who has let herself go a little. Whilst not actually smelling of wee, the club has a ramshackle atmosphere, and the ground, where the Tons have played since 1879, gives no hint that Clapton were one of the great pioneers of amateur and, indeed, international football.

At some of the fine old amateur clubs (Hendon and Bromley, for example) you can tell that large crowds once gathered. Dulwich Hamlet's old ground, a stone's throw away from their current modern stadium, was the best example – a cavernous ground capable of accommodating many thousands of spectators. By the late '80s Hamlet were struggling on crowds of around 200 in a stadium once capable of holding up to 30,000. The club did the sensible thing and sold the ground to a supermarket, who, as part of the deal, constructed them a new, smaller stadium a free-kick away from the old site.

Clapton's successes, however, came in the days before the attendance explosion of the '30s. The Old Spotted Dog holds barely 2,000, a capacity which has changed little in their long history. In fact there is little evidence to show that a once-great club plays here: there is no discernible legacy.

Formed in 1877 as Downs FC, Clapton moved in to Lea Bridge Road, later the headquarters of Leyton in their various guises, before taking up residence on a patch of ground behind the Old Spotted Dog pub in 1879. Eleven years later they became the first British club to play on the Continent, travelling to Antwerp to defeat a Belgian Select XI 7–0. The Tons were instrumental in the conception of the Southern League in response to the professional Football League in the north of England at the turn of the century, and soon afterwards they became founder members of the Isthmian League, where they have remained ever since to become the only club to boast continuous membership. In their heyday during the first quarter of the century, Clapton appeared in six FA Amateur Cup finals, winning five of them, won two league titles and finished as runners-up on four occasions. Their honours board reveals that the club has provided more full England internationals than amateur internationals.

Today, Clapton are members of the Ryman League Third Division, the lowest of the Isthmian League's four sections. The golden age of amateur football is long gone, and there is little at the ground to hint at the club's glorious past. The Ryman logo on the cover of the programme is larger than the name of the club itself.

Whilst Wadham Lodge is a modern stadium which illustrates the ambition of the club that plays there, the Old Spotted Dog reveals a club happy with its lot. There is a tiny stand and some limited covered accommodation on the opposite touchline, with the rest of the ground consisting mainly of tufty grass banking. Suburban semis peer through the trees around the old ground.

The club shop, closed this afternoon, is the size and shape of your average sentry box. Apparently, two people run it. God knows how they both get in there. The boardroom is a portakabin at the side of the pitch, where stewed tea and curly sandwiches are provided for the officials of visiting clubs by men in shirtsleeves and club ties.

In the clubhouse, a dark, draughty place with no windows, the sound of Sky Sports cannons inaudibly off the bare walls, with the pictures shown on a fabric screen full of holes. Ten minutes before kick-off it is still possible to walk straight up to the bar and be served without fighting through a crowd of people. The rolls have all gone though.

When the teams take the field, as they have done there for the past 119 years, it appears that the red-and-white striped shirts in which Clapton teams have always played have been shoved in the wash with the black shorts and socks. The white has turned a dull grey. Tilbury, meanwhile, run out in pristine black-and-white quartered shirts which don't quite match their red shorts and socks. Jeff Banks would have fainted, but in the Ryman League Third Division colour co-ordination, jacquard weaves and ecru are all foreign terms. Thank goodness.

Tilbury have a young squad, with most players in their early twenties. Their start to the season has been indifferent, whilst Clapton occupy second place in the table. The home side average nearly three goals per game, with the twin strike force of Gary Richeford and Adrian Allen contributing 14 of the Tons' 17 goals so far in the campaign. The visitors have managed just five goals all season.

Tilbury's history is nowhere near as illustrious as their hosts'. Their one achievement of note was a run to the third round of the FA Cup in 1978, where a visit to the Victoria Ground saw Garth Crooks, Howard Kendall et al. give First Division Stoke City a 3–0 win. It was quite a run, given that the Dockers had progressed from the extra preliminary round. Their squad now consists in the main of players drawn from Sunday football, perhaps a legacy of the fact that the club have spent most of their money converting their St Chad's Road ground from a run-down hotch-potch where the icy wind whips in from the Thames estuary into a smart little stadium where the icy wind whips in from the Thames estuary.

This being something of a local derby, the visitors are well represented in the sparse crowd. Behind the goal it appears that an entire family has gathered, from grandmother down to babe in arms. As the game commences, Tilbury belie their lowly status in the table by swarming forward at every opportunity. Early in the game, Clapton's keeper Dean Mann turns a long-range shot on to the crossbar, which is followed by two more efforts that have the Clapton skipper scrambling the ball out from under the bar. 'Looks like they've spotted your weakness, keeper,' says the dad of the Tilbury family. Or it could have been uncle, I suppose. Mann is a vocal goalkeeper with a voice that sounds as though it emanates from the bowels of hell, making Rod Stewart sound like Celine Dion. He is dressed from head to foot in black, and I look for cloven hooves, but his boots give little away.

'Lino, why are you there?' he roars at the referee's assistant (I still say I saw flames coming out of his mouth as he said it), who is dallying near the penalty area when the rest of the players are on the halfway line awaiting his clearance. Fixed in the steely gaze of Beelzebub, the linesman swallows and replies 'Erm, looking for offsides?' before legging it towards the halfway line. Dean Mann. Demon. Hmmm, alert a priest, I think I'm on to something here.

Clapton create one chance of note: a shot from Allen which is tipped over the bar by the Tilbury goalkeeper Jamie Orman. Shortly before half-time, however, and totally against the run of play, Clapton's Gary Richeford latches on to a through ball from the magnificently named Tony Mighty to slot the ball under the advancing goalkeeper and give the Tons an undeserved lead to take into the break.

Early in the second half, Clapton double their advantage with a brilliant free-kick from James King which curls around the wall, past the full-length dive of Orman and into the bottom of the net. It is a goal which kills off the game for Tilbury, who certainly deserve more. Despite building well through the midfield, they can find no way through the home defence. Lucifer in goal, refreshed no doubt by the live baby he consumed in the dressing-room at half-time, has an easy time of it, fielding backpasses, watching shots sail over the bar and plotting the fall of Christendom.

With a few minutes remaining, Tilbury's Kevin Clark chases a lost cause which is easily fielded by the man in black and aims a few choice comments at the Clapton keeper. Whatever it is he says (maybe it's in Latin?), it causes Beelzebub to throw his head back and laugh uproariously.

The final whistle goes, and one of the game's most famous names goes into the draw for the second qualifying round. It is hard on Tilbury, who looked the better side for much of the game until they conceded two quick goals and ran out of ideas. But the 120th season of FA Cup football chugs on for Clapton. Two small boys run on to the pitch and start kicking a ball around in the goalmouth. As the boardroom door creaks ajar, pictures of men with handlebar moustaches and knickerbockers look through the gap approvingly.

The Hackney Empire

Sunday Morning on the Marshes

In 527 AD, the London-based Saxon leader Erchewin rebelled against his king, Octa. Octa, on finding out Erchewin's highfalutin ideas, was understandably a little put out. He immediately assembled his army of 15,000 at Rochester and sailed up towards the metropolis. Erchewin's hordes met him in what is now the heart of east London, and the Battle of Hackney saw Erchewin's forces triumphant at the cost of thousands of lives.

Today the site of that battle regularly plays host to what are minor skirmishes compared to that bloody day 1,500 years ago, as each weekend thousands of men take to that field again. Not in the name of a Saxon king, but instead in the name of the beautiful game, on the pitches of Hackney Marshes.

The vast area of grassland that makes up the Marshes became a centre for recreation in the early eighteenth century. A 1791 bull-baiting contest there once attracted 3,000 people. London County Council bought the 350-acre site in 1893 to provide facilities for sport and leisure, and now over 120 football pitches cover the grassland throughout the winter.

Well, 120 pitches, 22 players on each. That works out at 2,640 people playing football if the Marshes are running to their capacity. If they're full morning and afternoon, over 5,000 footballers thunder around the east London home of football. I'm glad I'm not the one who mops out the dressing-rooms after that lot have packed up and gone home. Today, however, a hot August morning, the Marshes are nowhere near full. Most of the Sunday leagues haven't started yet, so a few pre-season friendlies are dotted around the vast expanse. Team-mates sit on each other's shoulders fastening goalnets to crossbars, whilst model aeroplanes buzz around the sky. A couple of people walk dogs around the perimeter. In the distance, Canary Wharf gradually becomes visible as the sun burns through the morning haze. In one goalmouth a man takes pot shots at his eight-year-old son, who has no chance of stopping them. He shoots, he scores, and he hurtles around the goalmouth in the aeroplane-style celebration made famous by John Fashanu. The little boy wearily trots away to retrieve the ball, a diminutive stooge to dad's unfulfilled fantasies. A couple of girlfriends stand chatting, the sun glinting from their sunglasses, the breeze gently shifting their cotton blouses. It's still high summer, but the Sunday football season is almost upon us again.

Hugh Vivian, a 34-year-old goalkeeper from Wood Green, has played on the Marshes for most of his Sunday football career. Today he is commencing what will be his last game here for at least a couple of years. For, as North London Olympians, the team for whom the Hackney schoolteacher has kept goal for the past five years, take on The Simons in a pre-season friendly, Hugh's cases are packed and placed by the front door in preparation for a two-year stint working for Voluntary Services Overseas. Through choice, Hugh is giving up his job at a Hackney primary school and leaving his long-term girlfriend and his beloved Leyton Orient behind to live and work in Ethiopia. Rumour has it his house won't have a toilet. Yep, goalkeepers are crazy.

'I've always been a goalkeeper, ever since primary school,' he tells me in the quiet sitting-room of his house in the shadow of Alexandra Palace. 'I played in goal for my junior-school team and I was the only one in the playground prepared to dive on the concrete.'

After keeping TCP and Elastoplast in business during his youth, Hugh played for a number of teams in north London before arriving at North London Olympians in 1993. He's even played, whisper it, Saturday football.

'Yes, there were times when I played on Saturday afternoons. I played for the third team of a club in the Southern Amateur League when I was younger, then I changed to the Enfield Alliance, which was quite a good standard – players from the Premier Division of the Barnet Sunday League played in the Enfield Alliance. It was good football, and you were often up against semi-pro players. I remember playing in a game where we had a player who was on Orient's books at the time, a full-time pro. He made a big difference, and I think we won 8–0. The other team put in a complaint, because he was obviously registered with another club, and we were chucked out of the cup for that. I'm pretty sure that Orient didn't know he was playing. Still, I enjoyed that game. I had nothing to do except watch.

'Anyway, I was doing a teaching practice at a school in Tottenham about five years ago, and the boyfriend of the teacher whose class I was working with played for this team and they needed a goalkeeper. I played a game to fill in for them and they were pretty impressed: they'd never seen a goalkeeeper who could not only catch the ball but call for it as well.'

The Olympians play most of their matches on Hackney Marshes, the rest at the Douglas Eyre Sports Centre in Walthamstow. Such an arrangement certainly negates home advantage.

'In the Southern Amateur League you play against bank teams and insurance companies all over the place, even south London, places like Bromley. We played on some lovely grounds. The only trouble was that if you were kicking off at half-one, two o'clock, you'd have to meet up at about eleven. Then the rest of them want to stop off for some booze on the way back, or whatever, and you get back about nine o'clock and you're all pissed. It ended up taking up the whole day. That's why I like playing on Sundays. What else would you do on a Sunday morning apart from sleep?

'I suppose it's a bit of a drawback if you're out on the Saturday night and you think, oh God, I've got to play football tomorrow. But it's the best hangover cure there is, football. Most people who've been drinking all Saturday night can't do anything all day on the Sunday. But if you get up and go and play football, you feel terrible for the first half-hour but then you sober up, and by the end of the game you feel a lot better.'

When Messrs Merson, Gascoigne and Adams confessed to their drink problems, I'm sure I wasn't alone in thinking, 'How?' How did they manage to train every day and compete at the highest level if they were downing a bottle of whisky a day or whatever? Watching football under the influence is bad enough (I end up trying to watch through one eye, one hand inexpertly covering the unused one), but playing with a hangover is ten times worse. Your mouth is so dry that what spittle you can muster bounces when it hits the ground. Your legs are screaming for forgiveness as soon as you break into anything remotely approaching a sprint, and within minutes you're covered in that horrible, oily, greasy film of sweat that only a hangover can produce.

So when some of the country's top players admitted an alcohol problem, I was astounded that they had still managed to compete at the highest level. These are, after all, finely tuned athletes at the peak of fitness. Pour a bottle of gin over the engine of a Formula One car and it surely wouldn't get off the starting grid. Yet professional footballers seem to be able to carry on as normal.

'You know when people turn up drunk,' says Hugh. 'You can smell it on them. I've only done it two or three times, but once I was really pissed. I'd been drinking till about six in the morning and when I woke up I was far too drunk to play football. But I still staggered down there, and when the game started I couldn't read the bounce of the ball at all. It was bouncing over me, past me, everywhere. I just couldn't play at all.

'You sometimes see people turn up to matches with a can of Tennent's Super in their hands or whatever, but they don't last the pace. For the first ten minutes or so they're all aggressive and running around, but the next minute they can't even find their way back to the dressing-room.

'It's often exaggerated, though. Most people are just there for a run around and a bit of fun. It's escapism, really.'

Visit Hackney Marshes on any Sunday morning and you'll find teams and players of all shapes, sizes and ages. From veterans' teams to well-organised, super-fit youngsters, all football life is here.

'I've heard of people playing for years,' says Hugh. 'The school keeper at work has got a 47-year-old in his team. I remember one game on the Marshes, there was a guy from Trinidad – he was 65 and still playing. He looked really fit as well. He was just standing in the midfield, not running around, but it just shows you can go on forever really.

'Most teams tend to have a character of their own. You can come up against a middle-class team, you know, all talking about their Fantasy Football teams, or a young team who are all a bit naïve, charging around trying to fight everybody. There are Irish teams, black teams . . . all sorts, really. There's a team in our league who are all Angolan, and there's a Spanish, or at least Spanish-speaking, team as well. I speak a bit of Spanish, so when we played against them they didn't realise I could understand what they were calling me!

'But basically Sunday football is shoestring football. That's the main difference between Sunday football and Saturday football. When I was playing in the Southern Amateur League, they were all big clubs and associations with their own pitches and clubhouses. Those bank sides, there's some really big money there. But on Hackney Marshes all you have to do is rent a pitch, make sure you have enough to pay the ref, buy a couple of footballs, the kit and you're on your way. As long as you've got somebody prepared to do all the administration, that is.'

In the world of Sunday football, the qualifications for management are quite different from those in the professional game. Basically you need a big coat, a list of telephone numbers and a sharp knife to cut up the oranges.

'The ideal Sunday manager is someone with access to players. It's all very well having someone who knows about tactics and so on, but if you can't find 11 players you're stuck. A manager can have his own ideas about tactics, but most players at this level have their own way of playing and won't budge from that. You're not going to change them. But a manager can earn respect in Sunday football by bringing in quality players, whatever the formation you're playing.'

But with the media saturation of the modern game, tactical quirks and professional foibles do appear on the pitches of Hackney.

'Some of the latest fashions filter down straightaway. As a goalkeeper I've noticed that everyone's aiming high with penalties these days, going for the top corner. The Shearer penalty, I suppose you'd call it. After the World Cup I expect there'll be an increase in shirt-pulling and holding, because that was one of the main things to come out of the tournament and players on a Sunday will have seen that and want to copy it. Referees will get badgered more to apply the new rule changes, tackles from behind and all that.'

Of all the Sunday pastimes in Britain today, the Sunday referee's job must be the most thankless and, sometimes, the most dangerous. If you think refs in the Premier League are under pressure, it's nothing compared to what beleaguered officials come up against on a Sunday morning. All the frustrations of a bad week at work coupled with a slightly sore head from the previous night's excesses can sometimes lead to verbal and occasionally physical assaults on the man in black. Many a referee has been chased around the Marshes by angry players after a particularly eccentric decision.

'I've played in games where the referees are so weak it spoils the game,' says Hugh. 'In one match last year the ref gave a goal against us and I was convinced the ball hadn't crossed the line. I gave him loads of stick, followed him all the way to the halfway line and got myself booked. Then we had one at the other end and there's no way it went in. But because he'd given a dodgy one at the other end, he gave us a goal. You can tell that if you moan about a decision long enough and loud enough, eventually you'll get something back at the other end.

'Now I'm not usually like that, but I did get sent off last year. It was for handling outside the area, and because of the FIFA directive the other team were all shouting, "He's got to go," which isn't really on on a Sunday morning. It's expensive getting sent off, I soon discovered. Fifteen quid the fine is now.

'But you do get good referees as well. It's a real mixture. You end up getting to know who they are. You see the referee trotting out and you think, "Oh good, it's him." You know he's not going to give many offsides, or if you use the "f" word you're going to get booked, and you adjust accordingly. It's the same at every level, I suppose. Some are very good and you're often glad that they're there. But whether they're good or bad I always shake their hand at the end of the game. I mean, they're paid about fifteen pounds, but there are much easier ways of earning that, aren't there? If it wasn't for them you wouldn't have a game.

'Some of them don't look like they've ever played football. You know, they're really young and they obviously want to become Premiership referees eventually. But many of them are just ex-players who still enjoy running around on a Sunday morning. When you've actually played the game, it does make a difference. You're a bit more wise to what everyone is doing. Everyone in Sunday football has their own little way of, well, cheating, really, standing on toes or whatever, so somebody who's played the game knows what to look out for more than somebody who hasn't.'

North London Olympians have just been promoted to the First Division of the Camden Sunday League, and the match with The Simons (two divisions below) ended in a 6–4 victory. A second-half revival saw the Olympians overturn a 3–1 deficit in a game shortened due to a late kick-off and the fact that the Charity Shield was on the television that afternoon. If you ask me, they should have delayed the Charity Shield instead.

'It was a dreadful game,' says Hugh, whose slight figure was left cruelly exposed to the opposition's burly strikers by a defence who seemed to take a while to find their feet. In fact, it was almost as if they'd taken a while to find the right pitch. 'We were admittedly under strength, but we didn't seem to have a back four. We were all over the place. It was very pre-season, but I think we'll sort ourselves out. What with just going up to the First Division, what we don't want to do is go straight back down again. Mid-table is something we'd be happy with. Bobby, the secretary, reckons we'll win as many as we lose.

'There is a higher concentration of good teams in the First Division. In the Second Division you know there is going to be a proportion of teams who are crap. Also, if you're a good team and you go one or two goals up, a lot of teams give up – they can't be bothered trying to chase the game. You come across that less and less the higher you go, where the teams are more up for it.'

The playing fields of Hackney will seem a million miles away when Hugh Vivian leaves for Ethiopia and North London Olympians to their First Division fate.

'I'll take a couple of footballs with me,' he says, 'but I don't know what to expect. I've never heard of any Ethiopian teams, and I've never heard the national team mentioned in connection with the African

Nations Cup. I expect some of the big institutions like polytechnics will have a team, but I'll wait and see what happens. Maybe I'll end up organising a team myself.'

In the end, the Regional Education Board for whom he is working turns out to have a football team, and the introduction of a top European import causes quite a stir in the area, particularly with his, ah, temperamental performances at centre-back (his team already has a semi-professional goalkeeper, paid the princely sum of £7.50 a month). However, the team plays at a properly enclosed stadium, complete with grandstand.

'I've made my debut at the stadium,' he tells me down a crackly phone line, 'playing in the middle at the back. I think they've put me there because I'm the only one prepared to head a drop kick. We won our first game 2–0. It's a bit strange playing in a proper stadium in front of a crowd. In fact it's absolutely great. I'm even keeping up with the warm-up . . .

'I was in Addis Ababa recently and watched a league game between Guma Trading from Tigray and Ethiopian Electricity. It was a 1–1 draw, but there was hardly anyone watching. Apparently you have to go when one of the Addis teams is playing for any atmosphere. Unfortunately I missed my team's cup final while I was away. We lost on penalties after leading 2–0 – the other lot equalised in injury time, so it's just as well, I'd have probably cried. Still, I'm back in training now, and another tournament's looming. The pitch is much better now as it has been trampled flat and the tufty grass has gone, collected by small children for animal feed.'

As we'd left Hackney Marshes in August, the myriad matches kicking up clouds of dust and grass cuttings, I'd asked Hugh how he'd remember his Sunday mornings whilst he was away. Looking back across the fields where over the years he had won, lost, saved penalties, dropped crosses, thrown himself at the feet of oncoming strikers twice his size and bollocked his defence, he'd thought for a moment and said, 'It'll be an October morning. There'll have been a little overnight rain so the ball skims off the surface. And we'll win. That's how I'll remember it.'

As Hugh Vivian departs for pastures new, he is one of thousands with memories of football on Hackney Marshes. As the number of playing fields in the capital is gradually eroded by the greed of property developers and the demand for housing, here is one place that will hopefully forever be sacred to the game of football. The pitches are indelibly marked with the blood, sweat and tears of over a century of footballing endeavour. Should the unthinkable happen and building take place on Hackney Marshes, do not be surprised if the city whizzkids and stockbrokers who snap up the properties suddenly find their plush carpets studded with boot-shaped marks. May their dreams be disturbed by half-heard grunts, swearwords and the scratching of a ball hitting the back of the net, and the inexplicable smell of Deep Heat and sweaty socks. May their showers conk out at inconvenient moments and produce either icy shards or piping-hot torrents, but nothing in between.

They used to say that when Matt Busby looked out over the pitch at Old Trafford, he was watching the ghosts of the Munich team going through their paces. Herbert Chapman is still said to walk the marble halls of Highbury, his ghostly footsteps echoing through the night.

Walking across Hackney Marshes on a Sunday evening, as the sun sinks behind the trees, the ghosts of thousands of old footballers roam the fields. For here there have been more matches, more goals, more tackles, more sendings-off, more fights, more twisted ankles, more victories, more defeats, more spectacular strikes that will live long in the memories of those who scored them – and which become more spectacular with each telling – than any other patch of ground in the country. Every rule change, fad, kit style and tactic has made an appearance here since before the laws of the game were codified. When people speak of football shrines, discussions immediately focus on Wembley, Old Trafford, the Nou Camp or the San Siro. For me, however, this country's greatest shrine to the game can be found just off the A102 on the way to Leyton. As the tip of Canary Wharf winks at you from one side, the floodlights at Leyton Orient rise above the warehouses and industrial estates on the other.

The blood of Erchewin and Octa's soldiers has long since seeped into the clay. But the determination, the tenacity, the nervousness and the aggression they showed one and a half thousand years ago will continue long into the future. Only today these combatants wear bri-nylon, not chain mail.

Rites of Passage

Harrow Borough v. Thamesmead Town,

FA Cup Second Qualifying Round

The second qualifying round of the FA Cup is when the medium-sized big boys join in. The 66 Ryman, Unibond and Dr Marten's Premier Division sides (that's Isthmian, Northern Premier and Southern Leagues to you and me) all make their debuts in the competition across the country today. The Conference sides join the fray in the next round. Harrow, members of the Premier Division of the Ryman League, therefore play their first FA Cup game of the season. They wouldn't have been too disappointed with the draw either. Their opponents, Thamesmead Town, arrive at Earlsmead as members of the Kent League, some four levels below their opponents. A 3–0 victory over Horsham YMCA of the Ryman Second Division in the previous round earned them their place in the second qualifying round, quite a scalp for the Kent League side.

Whilst doubtless pleased to be drawn at home, Harrow have a reputation for bowing out of the FA Cup at the hands of smaller clubs. They have reached the first round proper only once, losing 3–1 to Newport County at Earlsmead in 1983, and in recent seasons have made their exit against Edgware, Burnham, Staines Town (twice), Berkhamsted Town (twice), Bracknell Town and Margate. They have made a poor start to the season and lie 19th in the Ryman League. They have, however, won two of their last three games.

Thamesmead, formed as recently as 1969, are something of a cup team. Frequent semi-finalists in the London Senior Cup and the Kent Senior Trophy, Mead also reached the last 16 of the FA Vase, when a crowd of over 800 watched them lose 2–1 to Canvey Island. Going into this game they lie fourth in the Kent League, already with games in hand over the clubs above them.

The potential, then, exists for a little bit of giant-killing. In the programme, editor Jim Rogers looks forward to the day when Harrow will be regarded as the minnows. 'Perhaps this will be our season,' he muses. 'Progress in this competition is good for obvious financial reasons, and also for the national media coverage it attracts.' For non-league clubs struggling to make ends meet, the chance of being knocked out by one of the minnows who've battled through the two previous rounds is one they'd rather avoid. On the other hand, sweeping aside one of the little clubs opens the way for a potentially money-spinning tie with a Conference club.

Earlsmead is the archetypal non-league ground. Given that most income comes not through the turnstiles but at the bar, the clubhouse is the dominant feature of the stadium, towering over one end of the ground. With gates hovering around the 200 mark, bar takings are an important factor in securing the financial future of the club. Harrow's clubhouse is open seven days a week, offering attractions such as 'top comedian Johnny Cassidy' and 'dancing to Onyx'. Over the tannoy at half-time, the irresistible attraction of live country-and-western music every Sunday is offered to tempt Harrovians from their Sunday lunch tables.

Inside the ground, there is a modest stand flanked by covered terracing down one side and a covered terrace on the opposite side of the pitch. Typically for this level of football, the stand is occupied by the officials of both clubs and those fans who prefer their football seated. The covered accommodation opposite is populated in the main by old men who have been watching the club for many years and who still feel that there are too many darkies in the game these days. They're quick, mind, you've got to give 'em that. The sound of casual racism and constant reminders that things were much better in the old days (you know, world wars, tuberculosis, all that sort of thing) is a familiar experience at every non-league ground at this level.

The next generation are there also, ready to step in and assume the mantle of the old 'uns as they die off. Normally in possession of vast bellies, these middle-aged men are usually dressed in anoraks, pressing small transistor radios to their ears. Pubescent boys hover around them, constantly demanding updates on the Premiership scores, thus the future of the 'popular side' is assured for years to come. The time will come when the middle-aged dad passes up to the level of the old 'un, abandons his anorak for a long overcoat, tweed scarf and flat cap, and passes his transistor radio down to junior. It is an emotional rite of passage, bringing tears to the eyes of those who witness it. However, junior has his own ritual to go through yet, in a different part of the ground.

Behind the goals stand those who have progressed through puberty to adolescence. Abandoning the familial ties which have previously bound them to the popular side, they no longer have to ask dad for the money for a can of Coke. They can now afford their own fully fledged burger. Standing behind the goal with their mates, they can posture, chant and applaud safe in the knowledge that they are unlikely to come up against a rival 'firm' capable of answering their catcalls with a sound twatting.

I did witness aggravation at a non-league ground once, during a power-charged Kent Senior Cup semi-final between Welling United and Bromley in the mid-'80s. A knot of teenagers appeared next to the Bromley fans behind the goal and began goading them. Not used to this, the Bromley contingent started mouthing back, but noticeably edged away towards the corners. Eventually a scuffle broke out, and it was again noticeable that the mouthiest Bromley fans were the ones hot-footing it away from the scene the fastest. In fact the one Bromley fan truly getting stuck in was a middle-aged man with glasses. I'm ashamed to admit that I did land a blow myself, as one teenager lined up a haymaker at my head. Thinking quickly, I aimed what was admittedly a girlie jab that wouldn't have knocked the skin off a rice pudding at my potential assailant, and as he stood shocked at the lack of force behind my limp-wristed attempt, I turned tail and was away on my toes. Later I was delighted to discover a slight mark on my fist, which I displayed with enthusiasm the next day at school, where there were people who may believe to this day that I really did take out five people that night. Chances are that the mark appeared more as a result of later fumbling in my pocket for my keys than the pansy swat I'd wafted at the Welling fan that evening. Eddie and Dougie Brimson needn't have been looking over their shoulders for me. Which they weren't, evidently.

Down here in the Ryman League it is still sometimes possible to observe the scarf-tied-around-the-wrist phenomenon popular at Football League grounds in the '70s. It is also noticeable how many of these 'crews' (there's usually just enough to 'crew' a small yacht) sport biker-style leather jackets and saggy jeans. The growth of the replica-shirt industry has also filtered down to this level. In a number of years, though, the leather jacket will be traded in for a pristine anorak with detachable hood and a V-neck pullover adorned with the club crest, and the replica shirt will be consigned to the bottom of the wardrobe.

The half-time ritual of changing ends is another feature unique to the non-league game: the lack of segregation and open-plan stadia mean that the non-league 'firms' can stand behind their opponents' goal throughout the game. Thus a fat, bald, long-haired or old goalkeeper can often find no respite from the ribbing and abuse for 90 minutes. At another non-league game back in the mists of time I can recall a Corby Town goalkeeper who dared to keep goal against Dartford with long, flowing locks. This, of course, made him a great big woman. I remember being amazed, and not a little impressed, by the number of euphemisms the Dartford crew came up with to describe the female genitalia which the Corby goalkeeper was endlessly encouraged to show them from within his shorts. Some I had not heard before, nor have I heard them since. It was a sterling performance, more memorable than the game, that's for sure. And, because they could change ends, the fans had the full 90 minutes to work on their repertoire.

Thus the whole lifespan of the non-league fan from schoolboy to grandfather can be mapped out.

It is particularly noticeable at this level that the crowd is almost entirely male. Of the 202 people at Earlsmead today, 200 are blokes. One of the women is Sarah, who took the photographs used in this book; the other seems to be the wife or girlfriend of one of the players. The rarity of seeing a female at the ground was clearly too much for one middle-aged Harrow fan. Whilst attempting a surreptitious glance at Sarah's rear, he walked clumsily and noisily into a dustbin, falling face first into a pile of spilled Coke tins and ketchup-stained serviettes. Tee-hee.

Once the game was under way, it became clear that Harrow were a little apprehensive of their lowly opponents. Whilst their approach play was neat and well organised, time and time again they either miscued in front of goal or were too nervous to shoot. John-Barrie Bates was the first offender, swinging a spectacular air-shot at a cross from the right, Charlie Brown-style, and ending up flat on his back on the six-yard line. Aidan O'Brien, Harrow's impressive right-back, came closest with a 30-yard effort which went just over the bar, but when Frank McCormack dribbled his way past three defenders until he reached the edge of the penalty area, only to scoop his shot way over the bar and out of the ground, it seemed like it could turn out to be one of those days. Despite being camped in the Thamesmead half, Harrow couldn't find the net.

Thamesmead were a typical county-standard league side: big lads at the back with large turning circles, stocky midfielders in the David Batty mould, and barrel-chested strikers dreaming of the perfect cross to thump into the net using the neck muscles they've developed specially for the occasion, which happens once a season. Thamesmead showed little trace of individual flair, but had developed into a tight, well-organised unit. Thus Harrow found them difficult to break down, and when John Lawford hit the post for the home side with a flick header shortly before the break, you could sense that Thamesmead were growing increasingly confident of earning a replay. The desperation was becoming evident as early as the first half when Harrow's centre-back Alan Paris berated his defensive partner Danny Nwaokolo with the words 'Stop running with it, just get rid of it!'.

The second half began with Harrow again laying siege to the visitors' goal. Lawford went close again, Paul Adolphe managed to miss an open goal and McCormack weaved his way through the whole defence only to pass the ball carefully about six feet the wrong side of the post. From their umpteenth corner, Pat Gavin, who once saved Northampton Town's league status with a late winner in a game against Shrewsbury Town that kept the Cobblers off the bottom of the Third Division, shaved the crossbar. All this in the first ten minutes of the second half. Finally the deadlock was broken as Aidan O'Brien powered in a header from a Paul Adolphe cross.

The relief was clearly visible, particularly when, ten minutes later, Thamesmead's Eddie Jones diverted another Adolphe cross past David King in the visitors' goal for the second, and decisive, goal of the game. From then on the result was never in doubt and Thamesmead were out of the cup. This made them a bit cross, and a few sulky challenges went in. No one could get near Otis Roberts in the 75th minute, though, as he cut into the penalty area on the right-hand side. With one drop of the shoulder he sent the entire defence, half his own team and several spectators the wrong way and was able to sidefoot the ball into the empty net. The goalkeeper, totally foxed by Roberts's shimmy, ended up on the halfway line.

Three-nil was, in the end, a fair result. Thamesmead had battled hard, but for Harrow the chance of a money-spinning tie was still there. If they are as profligate with their finishing as they were today, their opponents might as well give their goalkeeper the day off. But if Otis Roberts can reproduce that moment of genius that led to the third goal, Harrow could be in with a chance.

Saving London Fields

The London Football Association

and the Crisis Facing London's Pitches

Every weekend some 2,300 clubs take to the playing fields of the capital. That's over 50,000 players from Highbury to Clissold Park. In the same city, Tottenham entertain Manchester United whilst Grasshoppers Peckham take on Fishblood Stiffs. The honour of clubs as diverse as Chelsea, Fulham, Barnet, Haringey Borough, Hammersmith Academicals, Cheese In The Wind, Athletico Lard, Borussia Dirtbox and Effingham Bonsai Society is fought for on London's pitches every Saturday and Sunday.

While these myriad matches take place all over the metropolis, from all-seater stadia that can house the population of entire towns to windswept, dogshit-strewn patches of ground where the goalposts list alarmingly and the nets hang limp and lifeless, there is a small group of people beavering away in south-east London ensuring that everything's done by the rules. From processing the bookings accrued by Chestnut Trojans and Real Ale Madrid to ensuring that The Valley is free to stage a major London amateur final, just about everything goes through the offices of the London Football Association.

The headquarters of the administrative body for London football is tucked away in a suburban side street in Lewisham. If you walk along the terraced, bay-windowed, Victorian-style residences from the railway station, in an insignificant-looking side street opposite a car-repair garage is the whitewashed converted semi-detached house that the London Football Association calls home. It's an unassuming location for the nerve centre of the game in the capital.

The LFA is one of the largest of the 43 county football associations which report to the Football Association. The London association covers an area 12 miles in radius from Charing Cross Station, an area which takes in the 300 league and cup competitions under its jurisdiction.

The association was formed in 1882 by the game's pioneering administrators Lord Kinnaird and Charles W. Alcock, both major forces in the early development of association football. The current descendant of that impressive hierarchy is David Fowkes, a man in his forties whose neatly trimmed hair and moustache give him an almost military bearing. Fowkes was a keen amateur player, turning out for Middlesex House in the Wimbledon and District Football League for 19 years. An accomplished player, he played for the league's representative XI on a number of occasions. During his playing career he joined the league's management committee and soon rose to the position of secretary. He was made redundant from Barclays Bank, where he had worked since leaving school, in 1996, coincidentally just as the post of secretary of the London Football Association became vacant. On the recommendation of a colleague on the LFA Council, he applied successfully.

As we sit talking across his desk, beneath sepia photographs of long-forgotten London representative teams and a huge portrait of Wembley Stadium in the '50s, I realise that his position was once one of the most powerful in the game. Today, however, the balance of power has tilted firmly towards Lancaster Gate, leaving the county associations to deal with the nitty-gritty issues. Impressive trophies bend shelves around the office; huge plinths bear the names of great clubs of the past. Many of the cups are no longer competed for, as the big clubs gradually withdrew due to the increasing pressures of a modernising professional sport.

But the LFA has had its moments. With pride, Fowkes reminds me that the London Football Association's representative team was the first British team to reach a major European final. The UEFA Cup began life as a competition for European cities which regularly organised trade fairs. Known initially as the Fairs Cup, its full title was the International Industries Fairs Inter-Cities Cup. Snappy, eh?

As the competition was for cities rather than individual clubs, London's selection fell under the LFA's jurisdiction. Drawn in a group with Frankfurt and Basle, London progressed through a semi-final with Lausanne to reach the two-legged final, where their opponents were Barcelona. The first leg at Stamford Bridge drew a crowd of 45,000 to watch a London side featuring Jack Kelsey, Danny Blanchflower, Vic Groves, Johnny Haynes and Jimmy Greaves draw 2–2, only for them to lose the second leg 6–0 at the Nou Camp. Despite this brief glimpse of international glory, the London FA's work is largely unsung. Which is a pity, because without it and its ilk the game below professional level probably wouldn't function.

'We co-ordinate the activities of every club affiliated to us,' says Fowkes. 'We recruit and train referees and linesmen, and provide an arbitration service for appeals against red and yellow cards. Our jurisdiction runs up as high as senior amateur level: the Ryman League and London clubs in the Conference. The 12 London Football League and Premiership clubs also affiliate, but that's more to do with history and tradition than actual desire. We also run the most comprehensive training programme in the country and administer nine county cup competitions at adult level from the London Challenge Cup down.'

The London Challenge Cup demonstrates the polarisation of the game in the last 20 years. First awarded in 1908, the Challenge Cup was London's showpiece event. All the professional clubs fielded first teams. The first final saw Millwall overcome Leyton. Fulham, Tottenham Hotspur, Arsenal, Crystal Palace, Chelsea and West Ham United all won the trophy, but by the time the '60s arrived it had become a competition for reserve teams.

'Clubs could no longer fit the matches in, what with European commitments and so on,' says Fowkes, 'and the competition finished in 1974. Spurs beat Hayes 5–0 in the last final. We resurrected the tournament in 1991, though, for the senior semi-professional clubs. Boreham Wood beat Uxbridge in last year's final.

'We work very closely with the Football Association. I'm on a working party with the Home Counties Conference, who get together once a quarter. We have a representative on the FA Council and on the Referees' and FA Vase Committees. In fact, a couple of years ago the FA appointed a County Co-ordinator to liaise with all the county associations in the country to filter through ideas and issues to Lancaster Gate. Whilst we are free to make our own decisions, the FA are the governing body of the sport, so we are answerable to them.'

The London FA is a warren of committees and divisions, all dealing with the separate entities that make up a game of football, from referees to pitches, from discipline to arranging dates for cup matches. It's not a glamorous life by any stretch of the imagination, but without these committees of volunteers in all the areas of the game that are generally taken for granted, London football would descend into anarchy.

'Unfortunately our main point of conduct with our affiliated clubs is misconduct. Last season we processed 10,500 yellow cards and 2,200 sendings-off. I've noticed that whilst cautions are definitely on the increase, the number of red cards has stayed fairly consistent over recent seasons. The number of red cards works out at less than one per member club per season, which isn't too bad at all, really. Mind you, you have to bear in mind that a lot of games under our jurisdiction take place without referees. The Essex FA handled 19,000 cautions last year, but then they've got more referees than us.

'The lack of referees is a big problem. We encourage people from clubs to become referees – that way players who aren't getting a game can stay involved. But those we do persuade to take up the whistle often don't stick at it. We're finding retention to be a real problem. We lose refs either because they see refereeing as part of a vocational sporting qualification or because they're only interested in reffing their sons' or mates' games.'

Despite these problems, the membership of the LFA helps to demonstrate London's cultural diversity. London is a cosmopolitan city, and football is a game that crosses cultural boundaries. There are teams and leagues representing many of the ethnic and political groupings in the capital. Fowkes points to the existence of the London-based Turkish and Kurdish Football Federation and the Anglo-Italian League as proof of this. A Latin-American League operates every Sunday morning on Clapham Common, providing a feast of South American culture from football to music to cuisine. There are a number of Asian leagues, whose memberships are on the increase. Perhaps before too long Asian players will progress to the professional clubs. 'I see our duty as to encourage communities to play in an environment where they are happy,' says Fowkes of culturally exclusive clubs and leagues. 'But there is an FA regulation that prohibits the exclusion of players on grounds of race, which leads to a very complicated situation. We have no particular problem with it, but I think things will have to change if those competitions want to progress.

'People also come to London from other parts of Britain. There is an organisation called the Association of Provincial Supporters' Clubs in London which organises a league. All the teams play in the kits of their respective clubs. Some games can get quite heated – Manchester City against Manchester United, for example. You'd think it was the real thing!

'We also oversee the Inner City World Cup each year, which is a two-day competition where different groups are invited to play for their country. They usually have as many as 32 different nationalities, which shows how culturally diverse London is.'

For all the city's cultural attractions, London's fields are disappearing. As thousands continue to flock to the city only to find that the streets aren't paved with gold after all, playing fields are swallowed up for housing. It's a worrying trend. Over 5,000 playing fields have disappeared nationwide in the past 20 years. As David Conn points out in his excellent book *The Football Business*, London has the highest number of people per pitch in the country: just one football pitch for every 1,950 people. Sixteen per cent of London's pitches – that's 263 playing fields – are earmarked for development, compared to just one per cent in the rest of the country. And those playing fields which are surviving the cull struggle to maintain acceptable facilities.

'Only last Friday, myself and three committee members went to the House of Commons,' says Fowkes. 'We explained about the scandalous state of pitches in London – there are very few first-class facilities left for people to play on. London has a massive population crying out for things to do, so sport in general should be a priority. Facilities need to be supplied to local residents.

'We're trying to arrange for some of the money allotted to the Football Task Force to be authorised for use in places like Tower Hamlets and Lambeth. Many of these councils have done away with groundstaff and caretakers, so the buildings just get vandalised and the pitches fall into disrepair. People feel that if the local council aren't bothering, why should they?

'One of the priorities of the LFA is to keep facilities at a decent standard. We don't just want them improved, we want them maintained. The FA and other bodies are always emphasising their keenness for people to participate in sporting activities, but there's got to be some-where for people to take part.'

The situation is not helped by the huge changes taking place in junior football. Under the FA's Charter for Quality, 11-a-side matches will no longer take place at Under-10 level downwards. This is seen as the best way to develop individual technique: a nine-year-old who touches the ball twice in a match because there are so many kids playing on a huge pitch isn't going to learn a lot. So the FA has brought in a system of small-sided matches which need small pitches.

'We can put these pitches in the corners of parks, and put on lots of short matches, but it's not ideal. The corners of parks are usually lined with trees, and the surface isn't perfect. These pitches will be used more than the full-sized ones, but we've got few enough adult pitches as it is, without converting some into small-sized ones. After all, where will the kids play when it's time to move up to big pitches?

'The London Youth Football Association has made great strides in youth football, and I'm very optimistic about the future of the game in London. But I'm concerned about the way things are going with the facilities. It's going to reach crisis level before long.'

Football has never been more popular than it is today. As England aims to host the 2006 World Cup and every politician worth his or her salt nails his or her colours to the football flagpole, no one seems to be addressing the problems of the disappearing pitches. Obviously there are more PR points to be won by being photographed with Kevin Keegan than outside a graffiti-smeared, vandalised block of changing-rooms in a municipal park, but with nowhere to play, where are the David Beckhams of tomorrow going to practise their art? Surely someone can see the irony of people being unable to participate in the nation's most popular sport because there isn't anywhere for them to play?

Already, Fowkes can detect a decline in the amateur game. 'The numbers are just about static,' he says, 'but a lot of league numbers are down. I think this has a lot to do with the standard of the facilities and the difficulty in renting pitches because there are so few now.

'We'd love to make it free to play on public pitches but then there would be even less money available for the upkeep of grounds. Premiership clubs are run as businesses now, but we won't be going cap in hand to Arsenal and Spurs to ask them to contribute some of their millions. We've got 100–150,000 players dipping into their pockets for subs and match fees; that way they can see where their money's going rather than asking the big clubs to stump up the cash.'

Tony Adams, Ray Parlour, Jason Euell, even the big names of the Premiership once played on the municipal playing fields of the capital. That's where they started out, where they were spotted and whisked off to a glittering professional career. If those pitches disappear, where are their descendants going to be spotted? Where will they develop their skills and tactical awareness? Thousands of words are written and spoken about coaching techniques and bringing youngsters through. But these techniques need somewhere to develop. In 1998–99 London had six clubs in the FA Carling Premiership, easily the highest ratio for a comparable area. Yet the region is crying out for pitches.

The picture appears bleak. A diminishing number of pitches, run-down facilities, matches played without referees. The London FA is working hard to train referees and club administrators, but the real danger is lack of facilities. Despite the problems the LFA faces in this respect, however, Fowkes remains optimistic about the future of London football.

'Encouraging people to play the game has to be our main objective. It's down to us and local councils to ensure that the game remains healthy at grass-roots level. At the moment it's expensive – pitches, equipment, fees and so on – but people will always want to play football, and we'll be here working hard to improve facilities and keep them affordable.'

If property developers continue to devour the playing fields of London, David Fowkes might not have much of a game to oversee.

Stress Management

Grays Athletic v. Aldershot Town,

FA Cup Third Qualifying Round

Way back in the preliminary round, Andy Perkins of Leyton Pennant dreamed of a home draw against Aldershot Town. Instead he got Ware away. It was the bank manager overseeing the overdraft of Grays Athletic who read the draw for the third qualifying round with the most pleasure as the Ryman League First Division side from Bridge Road came out of the hat before their Premier Division opponents. The idea of anyone dreaming of a home tie with Aldershot may sound faintly ridiculous to most people, but in the grim reality of non-league football the Hampshire side are the name everyone hopes for in the qualifying rounds as the draws are made at Lancaster Gate.

I trust that for these earlier rounds the velvet bag is still used rather than the flimsy plastic tombola thing used for the televised draws. As a staunch traditionalist (I'm writing this with a quill pen dipped in ink – damn, the candle fat's stuck my tankard to the writing desk again), for me the showbiz jazzing-up of the FA Cup draw was one of the most heinous insults to the tradition of the game. The draw used to be sacred: it took place on a Monday morning, broadcast live on Radio Two. You could feel the stillness of the air in that little room inside Lancaster Gate; you could feel the weight of tradition that hung heavy as two old men scrabbled their hands around inside a velvet bag as we huddled around the radio in the playground. You could faintly hear the balls clacking together in the bag, and could almost sense the ghosts of Blackburn Olympic, Old Carthusians and the Royal Engineers watching over the solemn occasion. The people making the draw probably even played for them. The weight of history made their shoulders stoop.

Did the FA really think that this ceremony needed an injection of

61

pizzazz? A showbiz makeover? Did they really think that people were switching off halfway through in search of something more entertaining? Of course they weren't! You listened to the FA Cup draw to find out who was playing whom, not to be entertained! The solemnity and deliberate pronunciation of 'number 31 . . . Portsmouth . . . (clackety clackety clack) . . . will play number 62 . . . Bradford City or Bournemouth and Boscombe Athletic' gave the competition the gravitas on which it thrived. The fact that Liverpool, Manchester United, Rochdale and Telford United all held equal status somewhere in that velvet sack illustrated the very essence of the FA Cup. Now those clubs great and small, ancient and modern find themselves swilled around a cheap transparent plastic tombola by Rodney Marsh. And it's just not on. Wherever will it end? David Davies dropping on to one knee, spreading his arms wide and launching into a rendition of 'The Cup is a cabaret, old chum'?

Are we really thought of as being that thick that we need quips, vox pops and snazzy graphics to hold our attention for more than ten minutes while the draw is made? The draw provided some of the BBC's most compelling radio of the year. You could almost smell the oak panelling, feel the velvet bag under your fingernails. It didn't need celebrities plucked from the after-dinner circuit making tedious jokes about the old days ('Of course, the amazing thing about my goal in the 1980 final was, chortle, that I scored it with my head!'). It didn't need fans and managers in the audience watching the proceedings. It certainly didn't need Barry Fry putting his two penn'orth in whilst awaiting Peterborough's appearance from the tombola. Bring back Gordon McKeag and Sir Bert Millichip, and the bloke with the beard who stood between them shaking the bag. Now. Or I'll hold my breath until I die, see if I don't.

The Football Association, in its desire to assert itself as a major player in the entertainment industry, has stamped out the very things that make the FA Cup the greatest competition in the world: its history and tradition. Not content with pimping the competition to sponsors like an old whore, the Association tinkers with the sacred draw. I'm still holding my breath, by the way.

The demise and rise of football in Aldershot will no doubt inspire a rash of articles in the sports supplements if and when they make it back into the Football League. In March 1992, beset by financial disasters, the Shots played their final league fixture, against Cardiff City. It was the first time since Accrington Stanley that a club had left the Football League during a season.

By the beginning of the following season a new club had been formed, had secured the use of the old club's Recreation Ground and had been elected to the Isthmian League Third Division. When the vote was carried, I wonder if the league secretary picked up the phone to give them the good news and said to the rest of the committee, 'Look, I'm calling the Shots here.' No, you're right, he probably didn't.

Whilst the old club had often struggled to pull in 2,000 fans to watch league football, the new club found crowds nudging 3,000 clanking through the turnstiles to see the Shots take on the likes of Clapton and Kingsbury Town. That season they won the Third Division 18 points ahead of their nearest challenger, with promotion being attained again the following season. A third successive promotion was missed on goal difference, with the Shots remaining in the First Division for another two seasons. In 1997–98, however, the arrival of former Barking, Chesham United and Enfield manager George Borg led to the club winning the division by 11 points. Over 4,000 people attended their final home game against those unlikely crowd-pullers from Berkhamsted Town. The Shots now find themselves just two divisions away from a return to the Football League.

If their crowds at the Recreation Ground are relatively large, the Shots' away following can often quadruple their opponents' regular attendance. This is clearly in evidence this afternoon, as Grays' own Recreation Ground is probably the fullest it has been for some years. You can almost hear the pound signs going 'kerching' in the eyes of the programme editor as he writes 'I hope all you travelling fans, and our own, enjoy today's match'.

Grays Athletic are a club not short of a bob or two, mind. Their impressive clubhouse contains a number of bars and some excellent indoor sporting facilities. Their patrons are the Billings family, the estate of Ron Billings, a late eccentric millionaire from Fawkham in Kent who built a football ground and started a club, Corinthian, in his back garden just so his three sons could play. Corinthian eventually made it into the Kent League, with Billings attending matches in a shabby suit, the trousers held up with string.

It is also obvious that the club once sold off a hefty portion of the ground to developers, as the luxury flats that dominate one side of the pitch demonstrate. That side of the ground is cramped, overlooked by the flats whose balconies provide the best view in the ground. Expensive way of watching the match for nothing, though.

The home side are tucked nicely behind the leaders in the First Division of the Ryman League with games in hand. They've not won for three games, however. Aldershot, on the other hand, lie seventh in the

Premier Division and are unbeaten away from home. The chance of an upset is there: is Aldershot's desire to return to the Football League great enough for them to sacrifice a good cup run? Grays would certainly hope so, but the determined looks on the faces of the visitors and the hundreds of visiting fans behind the goal suggest that the Shots mean business.

The Aldershot team all look the same. Short, save for the obligatory big lads at the back, stocky and shaven-headed. Their play is aggressive, competitive and unspectacular, in the style of all George Borg teams. The Aldershot manager likes to build teams in his own image.

Borg had a long career in the non-league game with Carshalton Athletic and Barking, earning a reputation for being a bit of a hard man with a short fuse. He had notable success when he progressed into management with Barking, Chesham and Enfield, where no game was complete without a small explosion in the dugout after a hotly disputed coin toss had gone against Borg's side. This afternoon is no exception, as he bungees off the bench at the slightest provocation. And I mean slightest.

Barely four minutes had passed when Grays' lanky striker Vinny John kept up his record of scoring a goal in every game during the season so far. Unfortunately for him it was at the wrong end. Aldershot won a corner on the right, John took up a position at the near post and as the ball curled in towards him the temptation was too great. Messages were sent from his brain: inswinging corner, free header, right on the near post. Before the striker's grey matter had time to assess the orientation of the pitch, he had flicked a deft header on to the ground behind his own goal line. The horrible truth hit home as the ball bounced up into the netting, where pony-tailed goalkeeper Ian Brooks pounced upon it. The Grays striker's hands flew up to his head, and the travelling army erupted with joy. Borg was out of the dugout, this time dancing a curious pixie jig rather than looking for someone to punch. Strikers should not be allowed anywhere near their own penalty area. Especially when crosses are flying around. Asking one of your own strikers to defend a corner is like asking Bill Clinton to wait quietly in a room with the Spice Girls and a box of cigars. They just can't help themselves.

Shortly afterwards, Grays' Jamie Wallace, a ringer for Stan Collymore, caught Aldershot's Jason Chewins late, leaving him injured and, it must be said, whimpering like a girl. The referee waved play on. George Borg flung himself out of the dugout like he'd been twanged out of a catapult. He was boiling with such fury you could have comfortably run a small generator off him and indulged in a good half-hour's worth of pneumatic drilling. The ref was having none of it. Borg's apoplexy rubbed off on the crowd. An argument between a female Grays fan and a male visitor from Hampshire over the incident degenerated into personal abuse in no time, the man's rather uncharitable response to being shoved in the chest being 'Oh, go home and have a shave, love'. Borg eventually returned to the dugout looking mightily pissed off. If this had been a cartoon he'd have had a big black cloud over his head with lightning playing around his ears.

It was at this point I decided to head for the tea bar, thinking that, a quarter of an hour into the game, the coast would be clear. Not so. Faced with a crowd some five times their average attendance, the trio of volunteers were struggling to keep up with the demand. The queue snaked out of the door and about 30 yards along the side of the pitch. It took about 20 minutes to get into the bar itself, where I found myself faced by a poster advertising a 'Pre-Match Farting Competition' at future home games. I hope it was a joke. Behind the counter were a middle-aged woman with amnesia ('Cheeseburger and a tea please', 'Right you are, here's your two hot dogs and a bovril'), a man obviously struggling with a drink problem (picking up a can of Diet Coke, he took a huge swig, creased his face with disgust and spluttered, 'That's not bloody lager!') and Beryl, an elderly woman entrusted with the tea urn. At every cry of 'Two more teas, Beryl' she would obligingly fill two small poly-styrene cups, then waddle to the sink, fill a small plastic jug with water, waddle back and top up the urn. It sometimes took two or three trips. It took forever.

When I'd finally obtained my refreshments and left the tea bar, I impaled myself on the nose of Gary Abbott. 'Zissakewfer burgers?' asked the man renowned for having the largest, sharpest nose in the non-league game. 'Er, yeah, it starts back there,' I said, waggling my cheese-burger in a direction over his shoulder. I resisted the temptation to warn him that he could have someone's eye out with that thing because he's quite hard and I'm not. Abbott is Aldershot's leading goalscorer, missing today's game through injury. With a nose that makes Bob Cryer's from *The Bill* look cute and petite, Abbott is one of the Conference's leading scorers of all time. In spells with Welling United, Barnet and Enfield he has notched up over 100 goals in football's 'fifth division'. I'd seen him play many times in visits to non-league grounds and found that I was still a little in awe of a bloke trailing two small daughters around a non-league ground in south Essex in search of hamburgers. I'll never get used to meeting footballers.

By the time my nourishment odyssey was complete, the referee had blown for half-time. Curiously enough, given the number of FA Cup games and the number of referees arbitrating them, the whistle-blower for this game was the same man who had reffed the previous rounds at Leyton Pennant and Clapton. Three ties of the four I'd picked so far on no greater criterion than I fancied them, all officiated by the same man. So, Mr A.J. Conn of Royston, Herts, I promise I wasn't stalking you. I hope the presence of a bloke scribbling in a notebook accompanied by a woman brandishing a camera with a big lens at nearly every game you showed up at didn't cause you to think that the Inland Revenue was after you. In fact, to be honest, it was only by looking at the programmes later that I realised you'd been there at all. Don't they say that a good ref is one you don't notice? Ahem.

For the second half I took up a position among the Aldershot fans on the covered terrace alongside the seats. In the strictly adhered-to demographics of the non-league ground outlined in the previous round, I was amongst the older fans, those in long overcoats, scarves and flat caps and with pockets full of toffees. The Aldershot contingent differed from most clubs' only in the air of smug self-satisfaction that hung over them like a cloud. An air of patronising benevolence, firm in the knowledge as they are that they're not stopping long in this division. Grays' miskicks are greeted with a tut and a resigned shaking of the head, the hint of a smile tugging at the corners of their mouths. Goals are greeted with a quiet 'yes' and a small round of applause, as if their players have a right to notch them up at will. They don't get excited any more. How can you get excited about beating Bishop's Stortford or Staines Town when your rightful opponents are Preston North End or Leyton Orient?

An air of frustration crept amongst them, however, as their heroes dominated the game but continually tried to walk the ball over the goal line rather than actually have a shot. Aldershot's approach work was good, if a little overwrought. Short passes, good running off the ball – but the final delivery was always lacking. It made for dull watching, and George Borg knew it. A volley of swearwords was occasionally shot across the bows of his team, and his white hair looked from the opposite side of the ground as if someone was bouncing a ping-pong ball off the roof of the dugout as he rarely allowed his buttocks and the bench to become acquainted for too long. 'Georgie Borg's barmy army!' sang the visiting faithful behind the goal. They could have left off the 'army'.

Aldershot continued to press, but they couldn't provide the final pass. Grays, meanwhile, couldn't seem to get the ball out of defence. It appeared that they had been camped for so long in their own box that they'd forgotten how to get to the other end. A couple of players asked for directions.

As the game lurched uninspiringly towards full-time, Grays suddenly created a couple of chances. Unfortunately they fell to Vinny John. Danny Hayzelden's cross from the right found John unmarked on the far post but his header was directed straight at the ample girth of former Barnet keeper Gary Phillips in the visitors' goal. Minutes later, as the Shots stepped up for offside, John found himself clean through on his own, but with only Phillips to beat he scuffed his shot six feet wide of the goal. Out of the dugout flew George Borg. I swear that he turned a full somersault as he leapt off the bench and launched a tirade of abuse at his defence that contained swearwords I'm sure he'd made up himself and which left his defenders in a crumpled heap over by the far corner flag. Another lapse like that and I'm sure angry George would have pulled out a blunderbuss and fired grapeshot into the backsides of his errant players.

In the time added on for stoppages, mostly accounted for by a bizarre tussle between the Aldershot physio and a Grays player whom he shoved unceremoniously on to his backside as he dashed on to treat an injured player (even George Borg's backroom staff are told to get a stiff challenge in early to let the opposition know they're there, that's how hard they are at Aldershot), Grays created a couple more chances. But in the end poor old Vinny John's own goal put the First Division side out of the cup.

The Grays player's response to the physio's assault, by the way, was to toepunt his treatment bag across the pitch, scattering sprays, bandages and smelling salts across a wide area, for which he was booked. Mind you, it was the most enterprising bit of footwork displayed by the home side all afternoon.

The Aldershot players applauded their fans, and even Borg himself approached them behind the goal. As the fans made to run away, they realised he was smiling and stuck around to applaud him too. They were milking it a bit though.

Grays had certainly contributed goals to this season's competition, their five games in the tournament producing 23 of them, but their dream of progressing to the competition proper had disappeared. Bumper takings would have softened the blow, of course, and at least Beryl will be safe in the knowledge that her tea urn will never require so much refilling for the rest of the season.

Aldershot went on to meet local rivals Woking in the next round. They lost. George Borg's reaction was picked up on seismographs across the globe.

Left Foot under the Desk

Garry Nelson and the PFA

When I arrive at the Professional Footballers' Association office in London's Haymarket, Garry Nelson is already having a bad day and it's only a quarter past nine in the morning. Some conflict has arisen between the PFA and the company which produces the *Players' Journal*, the footballers' trade magazine, and the advertising in the PFA's brochure to accompany their annual gala dinner. A misunderstanding has arisen over a misguided fax message. As I sit outside his office, the words 'It's not really good enough, is it?' float out of the door on more than one occasion, tinged with a Thames estuary twang. Garry Nelson isn't happy. And I'm here to spend the whole day pumping him for information, getting in the way and asking questions at inappropriate times. He's going to love me.

Nelson played over 600 league matches in a career that began at Southend United and encompassed spells at Swindon Town, Plymouth Argyle, Brighton and Hove Albion, Notts County (on loan), Charlton Athletic and, finally, Torquay United. His game was characterised by tireless running. No one could accuse Garry Nelson of not trying. Even in the twilight of his playing career he would be chasing lost causes until the final whistle. For that reason he was popular with supporters at every club he called home.

Now he channels that boundless energy into his work as the PFA's commercial executive, looking after the business side of the Association as it attempts to modernise itself alongside the game whose players it represents. Although based in Manchester, the PFA has offices in London and Birmingham, and such is the progress being made that Nelson's operation is looking to move into bigger premises.

Formed in its current guise in 1907, the Professional Footballers' Association grew out of the club that is now probably the least likely location for a trade union to emerge, Manchester United. From early struggles against the restrictive 'retain and transfer' system that gave players no say in their careers, the organisation grew and grew until its greatest triumph in 1961 when Jimmy Hill helped to secure the abolition of the maximum wage. Under current secretary Gordon Taylor, the Association has had to move with the times.

Having recognised the need to go beyond contract negotiations and advising players whose careers have finished through injury or advancing years, the PFA has become a far more dynamic entity in the 1990s. It is now a proactive organisation rather than a reactive one.

'We do still deal mainly with enquiries and problems from the players,' says Nelson. 'Every day of the week there are problems with football clubs. I don't deal with that side of it myself, my immediate boss in Manchester Mick McGuire does. He deals with club secretaries every day, whether it be disciplinary matters, fines, technical, administrative or contractual problems, transfer issues, medical cover – there are so many things that arise, but the players know that they have the security of the PFA there to look after them. When the PFA calls on a football club, straight away they know that they're going to have to sit up and take notice of us.

'If you didn't have the PFA the system would be so open to abuse. Over on the Continent, there are some places where you can lose three matches and suddenly your contracts are worthless, you're all kicked out and they've gone out and found some new players. What we try to do is ensure that contracts are honoured, that clubs understand that when they give a player a contract they have to abide by it as much as the player does.'

Garry Nelson is probably one of the best-qualified people in the game to represent the organisation in such a way. As well as having a diploma in marketing and having been a PFA representative whilst a player at Charlton Athletic, his books *Left Foot Forward* and *Left Foot in the Grave* have become essential reading in this era of football literature. Taking up the baton from Eamonn Dunphy's '70s classic *Only a Game*, Nelson's diary-style tomes provide a warts-and-all look at the life of a professional footballer. Nelson never played in the Premiership or the old First Division, hence his first book is modestly subtitled 'A year in the life of a journeyman footballer'. The closest Nelson came to appearing in the top flight was as part of the Charlton Athletic team defeated in the play-off semi-finals by Crystal Palace in 1995. The second leg was his last game for the club.

I'd seen Nelson play for Charlton dozens of times from the terraces at

Upton Park and The Valley. I'd read his books. I knew his life story. I'd called him by his nickname, 'Nelse', along with my fellow fans. I know that he's an Everton supporter. I know the names of his children. He, of course, doesn't know me from Adam.

Having finished his call, Nelson appears at the door of the office and invites me in. He's polite and affable, even though today he could probably do without me being there. He asks me about this book, but as I begin to tell him it's soon clear that his attention has been caught by a piece of post on the table, and I drift falteringly to a halt. 'Don't worry, he always does that,' says his assistant, producing two cups of tea from what appears at first to be a wardrobe but turns out to be a tiny kitchen. The offices aren't exactly spacious.

I'd only ever seen Garry Nelson in football kit, but here he is in a shirt and tie; his suit jacket hangs in the corner. One of the first things I ask him is whether the adjustment from football to commuting was a difficult one.

'Oh yes, this is radically different. It was very difficult to make the transition, and I think you'll receive the same answer from any professional footballer, whatever they've done since they stopped playing. There are days when you're coming in on the train in your suit with your briefcase on your lap and you hate it, absolutely hate it. But there are days when you get a real buzz out of what you're doing.

'It's a very different routine. You're no longer gearing everything to the game at the end of the week, the exhilaration of it going well and you scoring the odd goal, and also the downside when things aren't going so smoothly and you're not playing well.

'Obviously as a footballer you have a lot of time off, some six to eight weeks in the summer, and it is one hell of a life. You don't realise how fantastic it is until you step out of it. I found it difficult to adjust and I like to think that I had prepared myself as much as I possibly could have done. But you can never prepare yourself fully. You can understand why it is so hard to adjust – there isn't really any kind of job that is as good as being a footballer, but you take that for granted and don't really appreciate it until it's gone.'

Nelson's books are underpinned by the impending final curtain on his playing career. A leg injury finally led to him hanging up his boots, a decision hastened by the job opportunity that arose at the PFA. Nelson was halfway through a two-year player-coach contract at Torquay United. He takes up the story.

'A former room-mate of mine from the time I was at Brighton told me that Brian Marwood, who did this job before me, was leaving and my name was being bandied about as a potential successor. But I still had a year to run on my contract at Torquay. I went to Manchester for an interview and was offered the job, on the proviso that I could sort things out satisfactorily at Torquay.

'I went to see the chairman and said look, you've got three people here on player-coach contracts, and none of us are really featuring as players because of injuries. I had a problem with my leg and wasn't going to be able to play a full season anyway. The chairman looked at the situation in two ways: it was a chance to save himself some money and it was also a great opportunity for myself. He also said that if I stayed and things weren't really going too well, I'd be out anyway. So it wasn't a case of oh, we really like what you're doing here, we don't want you to go, it was more to do with cost-cutting and not wanting me to miss out on a great opportunity.

'Another way I looked at it was the difference between a one-year contract at a Third Division football club and potentially a 30-year one with the PFA, so for me it wasn't too much of a difficult choice. In addition my wife hadn't settled too well in the West Country, particularly as my routine was very different as a player-coach from when I was just a player. A footballer has a lot of free time – you're often back home by lunchtime – whereas as a player-coach, as well as the training and playing, I was always off on scouting trips and dealing with this, that and the other, trekking all over the place.

'But yes, this is very different. You're used to being in an environment where you're out in the fresh air every day, running around being fit and healthy, and then you come into an environment like this. But I do consider myself very lucky: I'm still involved with the game, and whereas the average career as a player is eight years, I had 18. I didn't have any debilitating injuries or ever need major surgery. I didn't play at the level I'd have ideally liked to have done, but I spent much of my career just one rung below that, so yes, I was very lucky.'

Much of the PFA's work with the players involves advising them what to do in the event of a career-shortening injury or when a career reaches its natural conclusion. The Association can also provide financial assistance in times of hardship. As part of the attempt to assert a higher profile within the modern game, a major PR tool for the PFA is the new *Players' Journal*, a glossy bi-monthly magazine which attracted a great deal of attention when it was launched early in 1999. The media dismissed it as a blatant demonstration of how footballers earn more money than they know what to do with, as a crass manifestation of what is rotten at the core of the game. Nelson hands me a copy to peruse whilst he types a letter. As I flick through it, I see the advertisements include Porsche, Rolex, Cartier, personalised number plates and property companies both here and abroad. Also, inevitably, there are endless advertisements for golfing holidays and equipment. I comment that the magazine seems to be aimed at the top end of the profession. Immediately Nelson bristles and I know I've said the wrong thing. This is rapidly turning into *Left Foot in my Mouth*.

'What, you mean by looking at the adverts?' he replies with an impatience bordering on a sneer.

'Erm, yes,' I reply, sheepishly.

'Well how do you think the magazine is paid for? It goes out free to every member of the PFA, it's a top-class production and it's got to be paid for. Therefore the companies who advertise in it are basically paying for most of the costs. To do that you need to attract the higher-profile companies. You obviously haven't actually considered the content at all.'

Suitably admonished, I bury my head in the magazine for a while. Reading it, I feel like I'm an intruder on the private world of the professional footballer. Most of us have dreamed of being a part of that world at some stage, and reading the *Players' Journal* is about as close as the likes of me will get to understanding the footballer's way of life.

Studying the contents pages makes for a sobering experience. Between the ads for luxury car mats and four-wheel-drive vehicles are features underpinned by two feelings: fear and uncertainty. Three articles concern ex-players and what they have done since retirement: former Liverpool full-back Alan Kennedy writes about his introduction to the after-dinner-speaking circuit, ex-Charlton Athletic and Celtic defender Mark Reid talks of his new life as a driving instructor, whilst former Wimbledon striker Terry Gibson reveals that a chance remark by his young son led to him starting a business manufacturing bicycles painted in team colours. None of that trio had intended to go into their subsequent careers when they had quit playing. They all said they had hung up their boots without the remotest idea as to what they would do next.

A feature called 'Down and Out' deals with injury worries (this issue: the hamstring, in intricate and graphic detail). Aside from this there are articles covering the PFA's financial-management services, Masters League Football (a growth area for ex-pros, as demonstrated by the London tournament for retired stars that was shown live on Sky), a piece about the legal situation regarding intrusive journalists and photographers entitled 'Can I Thump Him?', and advice on how to make yourself more marketable to sponsors.

This last piece is one that really leads you into fantasy land. After all those daydreams of scoring the winner in the cup final, those 30-goal seasons you play out in your mind, for the real stars this is the real thing. 'You think you've made it,' it starts. Yes, yes I do! 'You've had a decent run in the first team [you're right, I have!], signed a new contract for the next five years and the endorsement companies are knocking on the door [they are, they are! Which reminds me, I must get a new battery for the doorbell]. It might sound obvious, but you're no good to anyone if you're not performing on the pitch. So can you play?' Well, er, no. Not exactly.

I try to suppress the small boy in me who spent hours signing top players for Charlton to build around my amazing goalscoring talents. (When my mum found season upon season of statistics neatly written out on countless pieces of paper – the season I led Charlton to the double, the season we won the European Cup and were given a wild-card entry into the World Cup because the team I'd assembled was so outstanding – she only took them into school to show my teacher how I was wasting my time when I should have been doing my homework.) As I do so, I come across one article which deals with that most notorious of breeds, the football agent.

'One of the biggest battles for us now is with agents,' says Nelson. 'It seems that everybody has to have an agent. It's like a fashion accessory, and lads are like lambs to the slaughter in many cases. They feel they have to have an agent because all their mates have one, but they don't really analyse the situation and look at all the implications. There are people there who have been attracted to the football honeypot and are running off with more than their fair share. Don't get me wrong, there are people out there who do excellent jobs for their players and they've come to the PFA at all the right times, but a lot of agents will say oh, I'll sort out this and that, but when it comes to issues like education, where they can't make any money, they send the player to the PFA. A lot of people are taking money out of the game but aren't prepared to put any back in. I do work closely with agents quite a lot of the time; they're a big part of the game and you can't ignore them.

'Generally we have to see agents as a kind of threat. Potentially any player they get is someone we've lost, and we don't see them as having a positive input into the game. Some of them are even out there actively rubbishing the PFA, because that's the only way they can get players on to their books and away from us.

'But on the flipside there are agents who do concede that we are a vital part of the game. We're the ones setting up pension schemes and so

Friday
April 12th 1996

SEMI DETACHED

3 Arenas with 50K of Sound

Musical Connoisseurs of House & Garage

DJs on the Night

Gary Delaney (Hard House Records)
Derrick Jay (Best of British)
DJ Ribbs (Movin House)
JJ Smiff & Pete Fearn (Dry Bar, Schneekys)

11pm 'till 5am

Live PA on the Night from Michelle & Revenue

Entrance **£12** on the door **£10** in advance

Ticket Outlets

HMV superstores, Tower Records, Black Market, Soho, Temptation – Bromley, White Label – Camberwell, GBs – Harlow, Dance Time – Enfield, Sound Zone – Basildon, Vinyl Rhythm – Southend, John Man – Canvey, Tribe – Ilford, Tribe – Hyper Hyper Kensington, Music Power – Ilford, Ard 2 Beat – Dartford, Vinyl Mania – Ealing, Freedom – Watford, Revolution – Grays Lakeside, Amen (The Barbers) – Bow E3, Hardhouse Records – Romford, Criminal Records – Walthamstow, Dry Bar – Loughton, Tart Records – Maidstone, Kent, Hummit Records – Chelsea Pie & Mash Shop – Rathbone Market.

Power House Waterden Road, London E15. For further information call
Ticket Hotline – 0181 533 2781 or 0973 719 935 or 0973 664 934

SEMI DETACHED

Sold on House

Power House

and Garage

on, and it's very important that the players have good medical cover, but the agent will only deal with the things that make money. I have to deal with them because the player has given them control over their affairs.'

Overall the *Players' Journal* is a fine example of the changing role of the PFA as the game becomes an increasingly big business. As the Association represents the most vital commodity within the game, the players, so it seeks to modernise itself in pace with the frantic developments of the modern age.

'The PFA's role has changed mainly because of the TV money,' says Nelson. 'As a union we've been around for over 90 years and have fought some pretty specific battles. First the maximum wage, and most recently the fight for the PFA to be involved with the TV deals, which was a lengthy process. We've had the battle over the rights of a player at the end of his contract to take freedom of contract – the Bosman ruling has had massive implications for the game. We balloted the players at the formation of the Premiership, which delayed its launch, over things like pension rights, and we received tremendous support. Because of the length of time we've been around, the support of the players and Gordon Taylor's standing in the game we remain a very strong collective force within football. The money that has come into the game and then to the PFA has enabled us to offer the members a much-improved all-round service.

'The PFA today is probably in the strongest position it has ever been in, but, as with anything, you can't afford to relax. You have to be constantly looking at strengths, weaknesses, opportunities and threats. There are a lot of opportunities in football now, but there are also a number of threats to our position. The escalation in players' salaries means that there will hopefully be a lot of players who will be set up for life once they've finished playing, and good luck to them. You have to ask if some of the things we've instigated are absolutely necessary for those players, but we do still have the firm support of the players at the top of the game who are in that position. Take the Alan Shearer/Neil Lennon incident a couple of years back: the PFA was able to use its influence to obtain the right verdict for Alan in that case. Dion Dublin was fined a couple of weeks' wages by Coventry when he was in negotiation with Aston Villa, and we were able to have that action rescinded.

'Clearly there are going to be some massive developments in the game over the next five years or so, and we have to make sure that the players still have a voice, no matter what they are or aren't earning. Besides, all these lads know that they could go out next Saturday and one tackle could change everything for them. If they've not been properly advised or set up financially, they could find themselves in a difficult situation. We have to make sure that we're in a strong position to help them out.

'We're under no illusions: we deal firmly in realities. When you consider that, as I've said, the average professional career lasts eight years, and that 75 per cent of 16-year-olds are out of the professional game by the time they turn 21, there are bound to be a lot of people who need looking after, people who aren't going to have long and lucrative careers in professional football.

'We're here for the good of the game as a whole. We haven't suddenly been attracted by the money going into football, whereas there are a lot of people involved in the game who will only remain involved as long as there is money to be made. We're here to look after the players, who, after all, are the most important aspect of the game. It's not the chairman's name that the supporters have on the backs of their shirts, is it?

'There are people under the impression that the players today are doing well enough not to need a body like us, but one glance at the history of industrial relations should tell you that there will always be disputes between owners, management and the shop-floor workers, which is what, in effect, the players are. For example, if the European Superleague does come about, there will have to be representation for the players in matters such as disciplinary procedures or with regard to contractual matters. There's recently been talk of FIFA moving every nation's season into line, all starting and finishing at the same time, and having a World Cup every two years instead of four. Now sooner or later somebody is going to have to consult the people who'll be doing all the toiling. After all, there will be some very, very tired footballers who aren't going to be able to produce the goods which attract the television, which in turn attracts the commercial money. You can't flog a horse too much; eventually it's going to collapse, isn't it?'

In preparation for the surely inevitable Superleague, the players' unions of a number of countries have come together under the inter-national banner of FIFPro, the Fédération Internationale des Footballers Professionnels. Twenty-eight players' associations are affiliated to FIFPro, which acts as an international federation for professional footballers. The expansion of the Champions' League from 1999 means that the victor-ious club will have played no fewer than 17 matches on top of their domestic commitments. FIFPro cites Peter Schmeichel's decision to quit Manchester United in search of a less hectic schedule as a high-profile example of the way the situation is developing for footballers at the top of their profession.

'Fortunately for us, Gordon Taylor is chair of FIFPro and is on FIFA's advisory committee. We have to ensure that the players are represented at the highest levels,' says Nelson.

'We have to be aware of opportunities like that which might arise, and be strong enough to stand up to the threats these sort of proposals throw up. We have the biggest professional league in the world here, so we must make sure that our membership has the best representation at all levels. We know that we can approach that membership and say look, this is the situation, do we want to go along with it or not? We can stand up collectively and say this is what we want done.' It's all a far cry from the days of Billy Meredith, Cliff Jones and others who have worked hard over the years to create the foundations for what the PFA has become.

But despite all the activity at the top of the game, the Association doesn't lose touch with its grass-roots rank and file.

'The players at the top are attracting commercial interests into the game by helping to make the Premiership one of the best leagues in the world. Even clubs gearing up to aim for the Premiership are attracting commercial interest. Football's status as a commercial enterprise has risen over the past 12 or 13 years, and there is still a great demand for football at the lower levels. What we have to try and do is ensure that all the money now swilling around the game is spent properly, in the interests not only of the professional game but also of the pyramid beneath. We want to develop the best footballers in the world, and you can only do that by raising the overall standard. That way the best kids become even better because they're coming up against quality opposition. You don't learn anything by beating teams 15–0, you learn from playing against other good players and by realising that you are actually better than them.'

The PFA is therefore very involved at the grass-roots level.

'We were the driving force behind the Football In The Community scheme which a million kids pass through each year all over the country. We're very proud of what that scheme achieves in conjunction with the Football Association, the Premier League and the Football League. Such is its potential we've managed to secure Adidas as a main sponsor for the next five years – they've realised that what we're doing is worth while and good for the future of the game. The idea isn't necessarily to unearth the next David Beckham or Ryan Giggs, it's basically to introduce young kids to football in their local environment. The parents then see their local club in a positive light and there's an incentive to go along and watch matches there.'

As well as the youngsters, the PFA is equally concerned with the welfare of ex-professionals. The *Players' Journal* encourages members to contact former colleagues with whom the Association has lost touch. We speak a week after the Past Masters tournament was held at Docklands Arena, where Nelson himself was a member of the Charlton Athletic team which made the final, only to lose to a Tottenham Hotspur side which was inspired by the still-majestic vision and touch of Glenn Hoddle. This was Hoddle's first public appearance since his dismissal as England's coach, and as I sit talking to Nelson, a fax comes through from Hoddle's agent thanking him for his sensitive handling of the erstwhile England boss.

The Past Masters was another event designed to raise the profile of the Association. The PFA logo, a natty green-and-gold design more marketable than the union's official crest, appeared all over the programme, the Arena and the live Sky coverage. All day Nelson fields telephone calls from players saying how much they enjoyed the evening (and then politely enquiring when they might receive their appearance fee).

'There was a great reaction to the event, as there was to the previous one held in Manchester. Sky were delighted with it, especially the fact that it all ran to time! There are similar events already being planned for Newcastle and Birmingham,' says Nelson.

'We're always pretty busy with events. We have our annual big golf classic, which is increasingly difficult to organise. With so many footballers also being keen golfers, we're inundated with people wanting to play, so you end up juggling people around a bit. One thing we do struggle with, though, is securing the higher-profile players, who obviously command the most interest in the event as a whole. Most of them have work commitments and you find yourself going through the agents. A standard letter goes out saying this is our golf event, we'd love you to play, but that's probably one of hundreds of letters the player receives. He passes it on to his agent, who passes it on to his secretary, and 20 or 30 letters come back just about unread, which is a shame.'

One recent development in the modern game has been the influx of foreign players into British football. Whereas some of these players have become heroes to supporters and brought a fresh perspective to the game, others have perhaps seen the opportunity for a lucrative season or two where they can earn a fortune without putting themselves out a great deal. Other players have arguably been brought over because they are cheaper options than home-grown talent. The PFA sees both sides of it.

'There are a lot of good and bad issues arising from the arrival of so many foreign players, but ultimately we have to remember that we are governed by European law. There is freedom of labour movement throughout the European Union, so if a club wishes to sign an overseas player there is nothing we can do about it.

'What we have striven to ensure is that when a player comes from a country outside the European Union, there are criteria in place regarding the quality of those players being brought in. Clearly we are all worried about restricted opportunities for young, up-and-coming players emerging through our system, and if there are too many foreign players it's going to have a detrimental effect on the national side. Like everything else, we have to strike a balance. At the moment there are some clubs who have embraced the freedom of movement wholeheartedly and signed as many foreign players as they can, but there are others who prefer to keep their squads to a more domestic level. At the moment I think the balance is just about right between the number of overseas players and the amount of home-grown talent getting regular football.

'The danger is that it becomes all-encompassing and you start getting players from further afield than the European Union who aren't really up to scratch, and the whole situation turns into a mess. At the moment, though, I think the positives outweigh the negatives.

'There are quite a few examples of people coming over here, milking it for a couple of years and then going away again without having done too much. But I think that the players who have come over here and done very well have seen their influence reflected in an improved standard of play. The fans have embraced them, they've brought over things like training techniques and diet, a professionalism associated with a change of culture – but, importantly, they haven't changed the pace of the game. It's still a very English game here that the overseas players have adapted to. It's still the most exciting, if not necessarily the most technical, football you will see. I sometimes tune in to the Italian games on Channel Four, and whilst the technique on show is excellent and you see some fantastic goals, the games are nowhere near as exciting as our own.'

Nelson sees the main danger of too many foreign imports as the effect on the national team. 'If you go outside the 22 players who are picked for the England squad,' he says, 'then there aren't a whole lot of choices because there simply aren't that many players who will be good enough. That's a little bit of a worrying trend but, as I have said, at the moment the positive aspects of the situation outnumber the negative ones. The danger is that it's all very well the foreign players coming here and teaching our players wonderful new techniques, but if those players then can't get into the first team they're not going to be able to put those techniques into practice.'

We speak just as the Department of Employment is attempting to block the transfer of Marian Pahars to Southampton on the grounds that Latvia, from where Pahars hails, is not a strong enough footballing nation to make the transfer viable. The PFA approves of the government's stance.

'Yes, I think we stand quite comfortably with that,' says Nelson. 'The criteria are that players from outside the European Union should be international-class players who are going to be considered for selection and are available to play in 75 per cent of matches. What we don't want to see is a drop in standards whereby an 18-year-old who has come up through the youth ranks isn't offered a contract at the end of it because somebody's been brought in from overseas.'

Nelson clearly enjoys his job. That afternoon, the editor of the PFA newsletter, a less glamorous publication than the *Journal*, drops into the office for a regular update from the PFA's commercial executive for the next issue. The discussion soon turns to football, with Nelson leaping up from his chair on a regular basis to demonstrate some incident from his playing career. Amidst the reminiscences, the pair discuss the response to a questionnaire sent out to Premier League clubs soliciting their opinions on the *Journal* and the newsletter. The response has been generally positive, although one Premier League club's form came back simply scrawled with the question 'Very nice, but how many millions is all this going to make us?'.

My mind is immediately cast back to a careers seminar at school, where someone very high up at a huge electronics company walked out in disgust when, after an intricate description of various career avenues in the industry, the first question he was asked from the floor was 'When do I get my first Porsche then?'. The Premiership club in question is not one of the leading ones, and Nelson points out that very few of their players will ever reach millionaire status. He is positive about the future of the game, however.

'There's never been a better time to be a talented footballer,' he says. 'In fact there's never been a better time to be a professional footballer full stop, because it is a great life. But with that lifestyle come the pressures peculiar to it: the heightened media attention. However, there are lads in the game now who will not have to worry too much about what they're going to do when they finish playing, as long as they're sensible and seek proper advice.

'I think there will be an awful lot of changes in the game over the next five years or so. Big business is very much involved, English football is being transmitted all over the world and the attention level focused on the game is higher than it has ever been before, so basically I say good luck to the lads who are making that sort of money. A lot of companies are making huge sums on the backs of those players, and no one criticises them for that, so why shouldn't they be properly rewarded for it?

'But we are not just there for those footballers, we're here for all footballers and ex-professional footballers, and we have to make sure we can offer the best possible service to footballers past, present and future.'

It's been a relatively quiet day for Garry Nelson, apart from having to put up with me hanging around the place like a man-to-man marker. It has been a valuable insight into the real world of the professional footballer, both at the very top and at journeyman level. The Professional Footballers' Association has been around for nearly a century, securing the best possible conditions for one of the most exclusive, coveted professions in the land. Most small boys, and some not-so-small boys, dream of playing professional football. Garry Nelson has done it, and he and the PFA have to deal with the nitty-gritty of that dream profession. It is an almost-unique career, one which is characterised by its brevity: in what other profession are you deemed past it by your mid-thirties? It is also a career which leaves you ill prepared for the world outside the game if you choose not to pursue management or coaching or some other aspect.

Whilst young players today are offered riches and opportunities they can scarcely have imagined, the PFA is there to rein them in and remind them of the need to secure an education, the need to think about the end of their careers. There have been too many stories of famous players forced to sell their hard-earned caps and medals to help make ends meet, although the fact that these tales are becoming less common is perhaps testament to the PFA's drive to track down ex-pros and remind them of the benefits and services associated with PFA membership.

Dolby Surrounded

Welling United v. Whyteleafe,

FA Cup Fourth Qualifying Round

The final qualifying round of the FA Cup was decimated by the monsoons that swept across Britain on the last weekend in October 1998. My original intention had been to take in the potentially thrilling encounter between Dagenham and Redbridge and Stevenage Borough at Dagenham's Victoria Road ground. Having persuaded my intended that, although we were moving house that day, my presence was unshakeably required in the East End of London and she would have to move everything herself until my return, I squelched off at lunchtime, pausing only to telephone the club to make sure the game was still on. Halfway through my journey, I thought it best to check again. As I stood dripping in a telephone kiosk in Stratford, a voice crackled down the line, rising above the hubbub of a busy clubhouse, 'Yes, mate, definitely on.'

My District Line train pulled into Barking station just in time to hear an announcement informing passengers that the Premiership encounter between Chelsea and Aston Villa had been called off due to the inclement conditions. I allowed myself a smug grin; the game I was going to see was going ahead, whilst the international fancy-dans of the Fulham Road couldn't cope with a bit of drizzle. Ah, the magic of the FA Cup. The train sat at Barking for a while, presumably to allow the tide to go out a bit on the tracks up ahead, until eventually the stations of east London came and went, half-glimpsed through the misted-up, rain-splattered windows. As I danced inelegantly around puddles which were hell-bent on achieving lake status before sundown at Dagenham East, I became aware that more people were entering the station than leaving it. A steady trickle of sodden figures were making their way wearily back to the station like wounded soldiers meandering back from the trenches in the First World War, the only difference being that this lot probably couldn't write decent poetry for toffee. Then I heard the fateful words: 'Game's off, mate.' I couldn't believe it. It was two o'clock. My latest call to the club had been at 1.40, and then the game had been 'definitely on'. How could this be?

Call me an old cynic, but I then overheard a conversation which gave me a clue. 'Is the clubhouse open?' asked one fan. 'Yeah, mate, it's absolutely packed,' came the reply. As I peered out at the grey, sodden skyscape from beneath the station canopy, a thought slowly trickled into my mind like the dribble of rainwater that was simultaneously meandering down my back hoping to settle in the waistband of my underpants. Dagenham and Redbridge are a well-supported Ryman League side. Stevenage Borough are a well-supported Conference side renowned for taking a large following away from home. Particularly in the FA Cup, a competition in which they had almost beaten one of the eventual finalists the previous season. The fourth qualifying round is traditionally a day that brings large crowds to the non-league grounds of England and Wales. A postponement will inevitably have the effect of reducing the attendance for the rearranged game, as fewer fans are likely to show up in midweek. A club like Dagenham can ill afford to have a blank Saturday, particularly one as potentially money-spinning as this one. So, tell everyone the game's definitely on, even though it's at least reasonably likely to be called off, and a large percentage of the crowd, especially those from the visiting club, are likely to patronise the clubhouse and ensure ringing tills for the afternoon. Hmmm, definitely on indeed.

I admit to being temporarily seduced by the image of a warm, subtly lit bar, where dripping anoraks hang by the door and steam rises from the damp clothes of the laughing, relaxed clientele. Comely serving wenches passing foaming pints across the counter with a ready smile complete a vision of East End hospitality. A trickle of water running down my neck brings me back to reality. Nah, sod them. They've dragged me here on the wettest day since Noah said 'Thank God, it bloody floats' and there's no football to see. If they think I'm going to cross their greedy palms with silver, they've got another think coming. With an almost audible 'harrumph', I hoist my waistband, put my nose in the air and squelch homeward. That'll show them.

Four days later I was still in a sulk with Dagenham and Redbridge, so decided to forgo the rearranged fixture with Stevenage and instead plumped for the tie between Welling United and Whyteleafe, also put off from the previous Saturday due to the biblical weather conditions.

Here was another opportunity to search for that elusive, ill-defined romance and magic that make the FA Cup the greatest club tournament in the world (according to the sponsors). Welling United were struggling near the foot of the Football Conference, whilst Whyteleafe were doing reasonably well in the Ryman League First Division, two divisions beneath their opponents. Whyteleafe had battled through from the first qualifying round with victories over Banstead Athletic, Bedford Town and Worthing to earn a place in the final qualifying round for the first time in their history, whilst Welling were playing their first game in the competition. The postponement of the original game meant that the teams already knew that the prize for the victors would be a trip to Bristol Rovers in the already-drawn first round proper, a decent incentive for both sides.

Welling United were formed as recently as 1963 by brothers Barrie and Graham Hobbins. Thirty-five years later, the Hobbinses still run Welling United, having seen them rise from an Under-15 parks team in the Eltham and District Junior League to a position one step away from the Football League. They shared facilities at Park View Road with the now-defunct Bexley United and, switching to Saturday football in 1971, commenced their inexorable rise up the non-league pyramid. From the Spartan League they moved into the Athenian League, and from there they progressed to the Southern League. In 1985–86 they won the Southern League by 23 points, earning promotion to the Conference barely a decade after leaving parks football behind. They had a stroke of luck in their first season in the top flight, however, when they finished third from bottom and faced a swift return to the Southern League. Fortunately for the Wings, Nuneaton Borough folded and they were reprieved. They've been in the Conference ever since, and in 1997–98 finished tenth, their highest position to date.

The Wings have a good record in the FA Cup, reaching the first round on six consecutive occasions in the '80s. Unbelievable though it seems, it's only a few years since they entertained Blackburn Rovers at tumble-down Park View Road in the FA Cup third round.

Welling have built up a strong relationship with their local professional club Charlton Athletic, after the Addicks' reserve side played their Combination fixtures at Park View Road during the club's enforced exile at Selhurst and Upton Parks. Charlton reserves still play many games there even though they have now returned to The Valley, and the traditional curtain-raiser to the season at Welling is a friendly with Charlton for the prestigious Kentish Times Trophy. Charlton usually win this fixture by five or six goals, with the 1998–99 encounter being given added spice by the Addicks' promotion to the FA Carling Premiership. On this occasion fans were advised to purchase tickets in advance, which I duly attempted to do, embarrassing myself severely in the process.

It was a sweltering, sunny day when I rolled up at the ground. Tickets were being sold by one of the Hobbinses from a table in a room above the bar. Passing through the door, and temporarily blinded after moving from brilliant sunshine to the darkness of the windowless, dimly lit bar, I inadvertently blundered into the curved crone mopping the floor just inside the doorway. 'Gaak!' she spluttered, almost swallowing the cigarette that adhered to her bottom lip. Gushing apologies, I asked her where I could buy tickets for the Charlton match.

'Yaanagaapthustaressonnerite,' she answered.

Thinking that she was choking as a result of our collision, I was about to give her a hearty thump on the back when I realised she was actually speaking. 'Erm, pardon?' I replied.

Raising her eyes to the ceiling – quite an achievement, given the pronounced curve in her spine – she enunciated, 'Yawana garp thusstairs, sonna rye innit.'

I smiled, shrugged and shook my head as if to say sorry, I am in fact a complete imbecile who has failed to grasp the simple instructions with which you are attempting to furnish me.

Plopping her mop into her bucket, and sloshing greasy, soapy water over her carpet slippers, she said the same thing again, this time very slowly. Obviously the directions had passed her lips so many times that day that she saw no further necessity for them to meet in the middle as she spoke. Finally the penny dropped. I was to go up the stairs, and it's on the right. Raising my forefinger and nodding vigorously to demonstrate my comprehension, I spun around and marched impressively through a door and into the ladies' toilet. I toyed with the idea of waiting in there until she'd gone, but eventually I emerged sheepishly, smiling weakly at her. To her credit, she didn't belabour me about the cranium with her mop but merely waggled it in the direction of the stairs that quite clearly led to the club office and had done ever since the place was built.

The balmy summer weather of early August had given way to a rainy November night at Park View Road. Having parted with an outrageous £1.30 for what appeared to be a selection of advertisements randomly plucked from the Yellow Pages with a list of teams on the back masquerading as a programme, I made for the blackboard upon which the team changes were being chalked.

Surveying the bedraggled collection of anorak-wearing beardies in bobble hats who had gathered with pens poised, the anorak-wearing beardy in a bobble hat with chalk poised to impart the information his audience craved commented loudly, 'Looks like we've got all the ground-hoppers in tonight.' Speak for yourself, pal. A murmur of consternation rose briefly from the gathering as there was some debate over which way round the two Watts appeared in the Welling line-up. Realising the confusion, the fount of all knowledge with the chalk soon established that it was Lew Watts at number two and Stuart Watts wearing 16 for the home side.

About half a dozen Whyteleafe fans had gathered behind one goal, all clad in replicas of Whyteleafe's rather fine green-and-white quartered shirts. Their shirt sponsor was, curiously, the *Sunday Sport*, perhaps due to the pair of tits that played in the heart of the visitors' defence. After the teams had emerged to a balloon-and-confetti reception from the Whyteleafe barmy army, Welling were allowed to carve through the visitors' back line at will. Darren Anderson was the worst culprit, a stocky defender who had possibly the worst first half of his career. There were just four minutes on the clock when Mark Cooper was allowed to rise unchallenged at the far post and head the home team into the lead.

Whyteleafe attempted to get back into the game but were reduced to a series of long shots that rarely troubled Glen Knight in the Welling goal. Their best chance was squandered when Paul Dillon cleverly dispossessed Welling's Dave McDonald on the edge of the penalty area, only to shoot embarrassingly wide with just Knight to beat.

At half-time the players trooped back to the dressing-rooms beneath the stand, on whose roof in large red letters are emblazoned the words 'San Siro'. This is not some John Beck-like attempt at motivation by the Welling club, rather it is the name of a local Alfa Romeo dealer who's taken out advertising space on the sloping roof of Welling's stand, prime advertising space considering the ground's location in Welling High Street. Perhaps Milan's super stadium could invest in a reciprocal arrangement and have 'Blackfen Cycle Centre (for all your bike and rollerskate needs)' painted on their roof. Or maybe a system could be introduced whereby clubs display the names of other teams' grounds around their own. If Welling can have the San Siro on their roof, how about Gigg Lane at the Stadio Delli Alpi? Or my favourite football-ground address, Canal Street, Runcorn, at the Stade de France?

In the second half Whyteleafe went at Welling a bit more, and the home side became increasingly frustrated. As did the supporters. You'd have thought that over ten years in the bottom half of the Conference would have given Welling fans a certain resigned humility. Not so – they were on the players' backs as soon as the opposition dared to venture into the Welling half of the field.

Inevitably, with 15 minutes to go Darren Anderson attoned for his dismal first-half performance by sending a thumping header into the top corner of the net. The Whyteleafe travelling support went berserk. So did the Welling supporters, but for different reasons. 'Hales out!' they sang at the beleaguered manager. 'What a load of rubbish!' they moaned. The Welling programme carries an advertisement inciting readers to 'help Bexley Council reduce and recycle your waste', complete with a 24-hour answerphone number. Presumably the answerphone was jammed with calls naming certain Welling players the day after this match.

The stalemate lasted barely five minutes, however, the home side reinstating their lead with an almost-identical Mark Hynes goal to their first. Five minutes beyond that, the same player sent in a speculative 25-yard lob that was too much for Danny Rose in the Whyteleafe goal, and Welling began to plan for their trip to the West Country.

The excitement wasn't over, though. In the dying minutes Welling's Tony Dolby sent Phil Dawson crashing into the advertisement hoardings with a dreadful challenge. Dawson received treatment, got up and waited for play to restart. The referee blew for the free-kick to be taken, but Dawson ran straight over the ball and attempted to strangle Dolby. Off Dawson went, much to the former Millwall player's amusement. When play commenced again, the visitors' Lee Cormack took up the baton from Dawson and launched a waist-high challenge at Dolby, being fortunate to escape with a booking.

So Welling went through to the competition proper, whilst Whyteleafe were left to reflect on their greatest ever FA Cup run. The first round beckoned – now the big boys loomed on the horizon. Welling would go out at Bristol Rovers and end the season in the relegation places despite drawing 0–0 at champions Cheltenham on the final day of the season. However, Welling found themselves reprieved again. Barrow's dire financial predicament led to them being expelled from the Conference and Welling, having finished in the highest relegation spot, were given the vacant place, just as they had been in 1987. Ironically, the team whose expulsion had spared them on that occasion, Nuneaton Borough, were promoted back to the Conference in 1999.

The qualifying stage of the tournament is now over. Hundreds of clubs have been eliminated even though it is still two rounds before the Premiership sides join in. Is the real fun about to start, or has it just finished in a blur of violence and temper at Park View Road?

Sing When You're Women

Arsenal Ladies FC

When Tony Adams led his double-winning Arsenal team through Islington in May 1998, an estimated quarter of a million people lined the streets. As the open-topped bus transporting Bergkamp, Seaman, Parlour and the rest wound its way from Highbury to Islington Town Hall for a slap-up feed and a few light ales, following close behind was an identical bus containing another victorious Arsenal team waggling trophies at the gathered masses of north London. For Arsène Wenger's charges were not the only double silverware winners based in Avenell Road that season. Indeed, the most successful Arsenal manager of recent times is neither Wenger nor George Graham, but Vic Akers of Arsenal Ladies FC.

In 1997–98 and 1998–99, Arsenal Ladies clinched the Women's FA Cup and National League Cup, missing out on a unique treble by three points in finishing runners-up to Everton and Croydon twice in succession in the National Premier League. The previous season Arsenal Ladies won the league at a canter and, indeed, have lost just four league games in the past three seasons. In all they have won the National Premier League three times since its inception in 1993, the League Cup five times and the FA Cup four times. Not a bad record for a team only 12 years old.

Three clubs dominate women's football: Arsenal, Doncaster Belles and Croydon (whose team sat behind the goal at the Women's FA Cup final at The Valley in 1999 hurling abuse at the Arsenal players – there's not a lot of love lost at the top of the women's game). Arsenal's results in 1998–99 included a 9–0 win at Ilkeston Town, victory by the same scoreline against Wolves in the League Cup and an 11–0 tonking of Chelsea in the FA Cup. The reserve team won every match save a friendly against an American team, which they drew. On four occasions the reserves chalked up double figures, with poor old Ipswich Town on the receiving end of 10–0 and 13–0 defeats.

A lot of men scoff at the women's game, but the football played in the Women's Premier League is of astonishing quality. In their 6–0 demolition of Ilkeston Town in April 1999, I watched an Arsenal side containing seven full England internationals, one Irish international and an England Under-21 international playing some fantastic football. The intricacy of the passing, the slick movement off the ball and the devastating finishing would astonish most casual observers. Any sniggering would have been extinguished a couple of minutes after the kick-off. Those men who chortle at the very thought of women who play football – and it is thankfully a diminishing band – would not stand a chance put in front of this Arsenal side.

A few years ago I played for a five-a-side team in a Thursday night league at a local sports centre. Our team wasn't very good. One night, as we pondered our tactics ('Hey, let's try passing to each other instead of the other team'), a diminutive young woman named Julie Ferrett strolled up with a pair of trainers slung over her shoulder and asked if she could turn out for our team. Why not, we thought, she certainly couldn't do any worse than us. And she was wearing a matching tracksuit top and trousers, which boded reasonably well.

Amid much pointing and laughter from the opposition, Julie took the field with us. They should at least have suspected something, given that our team didn't have a kit as such – we sported a motley collection of shorts, track pants, T-shirts and, well, anything short of full evening dress. We knew who our team-mates were more by the fact that anyone not wearing a matching shirt was one of our lot, hence well-placed passes to spectators, caretakers and the drinks machine were not uncommon. Julie, however, was resplendent in matching sky-blue shirt, shorts and socks.

The game began and Julie received the ball. A member of the opposition sauntered casually towards her with a half-smile on his face, ready to rob the ball like stealing a lollipop from a small child. In a blur, Julie had dropped her shoulder, ghosted past him and three other players and buried the ball in the back of the net with a shot of fearsome power. By the time the first defender had realised what had happened and turned around, Julie was trotting back past him to wait patiently for the restart. There were barely six seconds on the clock.

Julie Ferrett, you see, was a professional footballer, a Welsh international who played for half the year in Greece, the other half in America. She was back in England visiting her father, who refereed the five-a-side league, and just fancied a run out. It's probably not much of an accolade, I grant you, but Julie Ferrett is easily the best player I've ever played alongside. Well, it was more several yards behind, cheering loudly and making obscene gestures at the opposition as she rattled another one past a goalkeeper floundering in the net like a halibut on the deck of a trawler, but you know what I mean.

Julie played six matches for us over two Thursdays, hence at the end of the season our record was played 48, won 6, lost 42. Naturally we wanted to sign Julie on a more permanent basis, but our offer of half a lager match fee and a lift home in a battered Fiat Panda surprisingly wasn't enough to coax her from her jet-setting lifestyle. The fact that I was also a bit smitten by her (a woman who could play football with a skill and grace as rare as precious metal did odd things to the psyche of a football-mad, hopelessly romantic 18-year-old) almost raised the fee to a Bacardi and Coke and a bag of peanuts, but common sense prevailed.

I don't know where Julie is now, but ever since she waltzed in and out of the lives of the Orpington College English Re-sits five-a-side team with a ball glued to her toe I have held a great respect for women's football. And, in a life-imitates-art scene reminiscent of *Gregory's Girl*, the day she showed me the cartilage-operation scar on her knee as we shared a packet of Worcester Sauce crisps sitting in the swimming-pool viewing gallery formed an integral part of my adolescent development. The smell of chlorine still makes my heart skip a beat . . .

In women's football the emphasis is firmly on skill and technique. In the entire 90 minutes at Boreham Wood that day I saw only about two or three challenges that could be described as remotely approaching crunching. The pace of the game is noticeably slower than men's football, but this is more than compensated for by the standard of technique. Unfortunately, no more than 50 people had turned up to watch. Eight times that number roll up at the same ground to watch Boreham Wood huff, puff and grunt their way inelegantly through 90 minutes in the Ryman League. It's an incongruous situation for those who like to watch the game played as it should be.

Arsenal Ladies was founded in 1987, when Aylesbury Ladies was absorbed into the Arsenal bosom by the Highbury Community Liaison manager Vic Akers. The club now operates a first team, a reserve team and a third team, as well as putting out sides at Under-14 and Under-12 levels.

Against Ilkeston Town, the defence was marshalled and dominated by Faye White, who, at 20, is probably already heartily sick of being compared to Tony Adams. But what the hell, I'll do it anyway. Faye White is to Arsenal Ladies what Tony Adams is to the Arsenal men. She is a tall, positionally intelligent player, good in the air and with a talent for building attacks with a well-placed pass rather than hoofing the ball up the field. A regular England international, she was voted Premiership Player of the Year in 1998.

Up front, 31-year-old Marianne Spacey is probably one of the few vaguely familiar names in women's football. Another regular England international, Spacey is partnered in attack by the dreadlocked Rachel Yankey, a player who plays with an effervescent enthusiasm and who was a constant thorn in Ilkeston's side that afternoon. It was noticeable that even when they were six goals up, Arsenal were still working hard as if the game was still goalless.

Wearing a track up and down the left at wing-back was 28-year-old Clare Wheatley. Another England international, Wheatley missed the entire 1997–98 season with a cruciate-ligament injury but today showed no ill effects with her tireless endeavour. It's a good job she has so much energy, because she doubles up as the Arsenal Ladies development officer and co-ordinator, the only full-time employee at any of the women's premier clubs.

Clare Wheatley joined Arsenal in 1995, taking over the job in September 1997. She began playing seriously at the age of ten, but 'my mum says that from the moment I could walk I was kicking a ball'. Her break came whilst playing in a competition familiar to Londoners of a certain age, the Metropolitan Police five-a-sides, an annual tournament that involved schools and clubs from across the capital. 'My youth club reached the final,' says Wheatley, 'and a team there asked me to join them. We went on to win the London Youth Games. I joined Friends of Fulham after that, before leaving for Sheffield University and playing for Sheffield Wednesday. I came back to London and joined Chelsea, mainly because they were my local club. I heard Arsenal were holding trials, I came down, and I ended up playing my first game for them at Anfield, when we beat Liverpool 6–0.'

Wheatley is a busy woman. As well as dealing with the administration of the ladies' club, she fields numerous press enquiries and oversees the FA Centre of Excellence set up at Highbury as part of an FA plan to improve the women's game. She has an office in the impressive JVC Centre behind the South Stand at Highbury, where I met her one rainy Monday morning. We talked in a lounge overlooking the indoor arena where the women train twice a week. Such facilities would be the envy of most clubs, and it helps the players feel a part of the Arsenal club. It's a weird feeling – I'm talking to an England international, but one whose club matches attract no more than around 100 spectators.

'For a normal league match we get 100 to 150 people showing up, with up to 5,000 for a cup final. We play at Highbury a couple of times a year, groundstaff permitting, but obviously you lose a lot of the atmosphere playing at a nearly empty Premier League ground. We normally manage to squeeze in a game or two at the end of the season, but now the men's season is starting earlier than before, we don't know if the groundstaff will allow us to do it any more. David Dein has mentioned the possibility of us playing a match before one of the men's matches, which would be great. Tranmere and the New Den are nice to play at. They're big grounds but you still get a decent atmosphere.'

Arsenal's vice-chairman David Dein and the parent club are particularly supportive of the women's teams. It was Dein himself who approached Wheatley with the open-topped-bus idea, whilst the male players also show a keen interest in the fortunes of their female counterparts.

'The men's team is really supportive. For example, on our way back from last year's cup final, Alex Manninger rang us up to see how we got on. There is an awareness now, which is nice, really nice. It is a genuine acceptance of what we're doing. It used to be more of a PR thing but now everyone's wholeheartedly behind us.'

Unfortunately the interest hasn't extended to the supporters in terms of people actually turning up to matches.

'At the moment, a lot of Arsenal men's games are on Sundays, the same as ours,' says Wheatley, 'but even if they play on a Saturday, then Sunday is usually people's day off to stay at home. We do get a lot of publicity for our games – our fixtures are mentioned on the Jumbotron and we have a page in the programme. We even have announcements over the PA at half-time saying how we're doing.'

Perhaps the apathy stems from the fact that home games are played in the wilds of Boreham Wood, Hertfordshire. It's quite a way out of north London. But perhaps too women's football is still seen as something of a novelty, something not to be taken seriously as a sport. Sky now covers the Women's FA Cup final live, with the 1999 final attracting a crowd of over 6,000 to The Valley to see Arsenal beat Southampton 2–0, Wheatley scoring the second for the Gunners. But generally, media coverage of the game is sparse, although Pete Davies's *I Lost my Heart to the Belles* led to the *Playing the Field* television series. There is a column in the weekly newspaper *Sport First* and an excellent magazine devoted to women's football called *On the Ball*, but coverage in the general media is almost non-existent. The Sky coverage is an obvious bonus to the game, but the tone of the commentary and punditry often barely conceals the sniggers and innuendo.

It's a continuing frustration for those involved in the women's game, but the opening of the Football Association Centres of Excellence specifically for girls across the country is a step in the right direction. There are 20 such centres in England, one of which is based under Wheatley's auspices at Highbury. Fred Donnelly of the Arsenal coaching staff, responsible for the development of Stephen Hughes and others, has been appointed director of coaching, whilst Ladies' skipper Sian Williams also helps out. In a unique sponsorship deal, Nike have agreed to pump cash into the venture.

'The FA have established 20 Centres of Excellence around the country,' Wheatley tells me, 'but six of them are in London. There's our one, Barnet have one, Charlton, Millwall, Chelsea and Fulham have them, and I understand that Wimbledon are starting one too. It's down to individual clubs rather than geography. If a club put in a decent application and fulfil all the criteria, they receive the FA grant and away they go.'

The grant is only £15,000 over three years, but Arsenal clearly have a head start in terms of finance and facilities. 'At the moment we've got schemes at Under-12 and Under-14 levels, but we're looking at extending that to Under-10s and Under-16s, so it's a massive task. At the moment there are about 30 girls at the centre, each of whom needs her own logbook, development programme and theory notes.

'We're looking at an overall talent plan – developing the grass-roots, getting into schools, right the way up to the élite. We're putting the best girls into the Centre of Excellence – and they come here from as far afield as Croydon and Milton Keynes – to develop them for the future.'

Yet Arsenal have been developing young women players for a number of years. 'We've operated Under-12 and Under-14 teams for about a decade now. There are a couple of girls in the first team who have come all the way through the system. Although the title wasn't in use at the time, you could say that we've always been a centre of excellence.'

Wheatley already perceives an increase in standards, a situation she feels will improve dramatically over the next few years.

'No disrespect to them, but take Barnet. At their Centre of Excellence there are probably only one or two girls who could really be considered as excellent, but they are the best players around at the moment. Obviously as the years go by, standards all round will improve. I'm even receiving applications from six- and seven-year-olds, and the youngest girl we have at the moment is eight.'

This increasing opportunity for girls to take up the game is a far cry from Wheatley's generation, who had to badger reluctant PE teachers to allow them to kick a ball around instead of trying to throw one through a hoop. The upswing in standards from the Centre of Excellence scheme will hopefully open up the women's game at the top level a little more. For the likes of Arsenal, at the moment the challenges are few and far between, so far ahead of the pack are they.

'The reserve section of the women's game has just been taken over by the FA,' Wheatley explains. 'They've split the reserve teams of Premier League clubs and put them into local leagues. We've been put into this league for reserve teams north of the river. We're hammering other teams 11 or 12–0 because they've only had reserve teams for a year or so. We've had a reserve team for years. It's penalised us because we've been taken out of our old league where we were getting good games against decent first teams and put into this new one where we're up against teams who aren't as good yet. We've got two internationals in the reserves at the moment coming back from injury, and they're not really getting a decent run out.' It's hard to imagine Dennis Bergkamp coming back from injury with 90 minutes against the Rose and Crown at Wormwood Scrubs on a Sunday morning.

However, whilst the frustration of being held back by the state of the women's game obviously bothers Wheatley and Arsenal, she realises that it's only a matter of time before the rest of the game catches up.

'For the next three or four years there will really be only about four teams in with a shout of winning the league: ourselves, Croydon, Doncaster Belles and Millwall Lionesses, although they've lost a few players and staff recently and have faded a bit. Everton won the league last year, but they're about fourth from bottom now. That situation will change because the game is definitely improving all round, all over the country.

'We beat Ilkeston 9–0 this season, but it used to be worse. Arsenal, Croydon, Doncaster and Millwall would be hammering other teams 10, 11, 12–0 on a regular basis, but now a good win is four or five. It is definitely levelling off a bit in the Premier Division. Other teams are now developing their own youth teams, which they didn't have before, so technically clubs are becoming stronger.' Long gone are the occasions such as that which took place in 1983 when Norwich City beat Milton Keynes 40–0, Linda Curl netting 22 times.

'There's still quite a gulf, though, between top and bottom clubs. I mean, we receive interest from everywhere. We have two girls in the squad who've come over from Ireland to play for us, there's a girl from Australia, two from America, a Spanish goalkeeper, a girl from Italy. I get e-mails from all over. We even had a girl fly over from California for a trial at our Centre of Excellence. She literally came over for the trial and flew back the next day. She's only 14, and she's got a British passport so she could come back and play for England. We've got a house around the corner which Arsenal owns. We put the girls up there and help them find a job if we can.'

Although the British game is improving, it still lags behind the United States and much of Europe in terms of standards and development. It has been restricted by old-fashioned attitudes and the petty bureaucracy of an administration governed until recently by old men. The Women's FA was not launched until 1969. As recently as 1962 the Football Association had openly opposed women's football. The first, unofficial, women's World Cup was held in Italy in 1970, with England represented by Chiltern Valley of the East Midlands Ladies' Alliance. A year later, Chiltern travelled to another World Cup in Mexico, which was altogether less enlightened than your average *Benny Hill Show*. The goals were painted pink, beauty parlours were put into the dressing-rooms and teams were invited to wear hot pants and skimpy blouses rather than football shirts and shorts.

The FA reluctantly admitted the WFA in 1971, whilst Ted Croker, who took over as FA secretary in 1973, said it was 'unnatural' for women to play football. Despite these setbacks, England reached the final of the first European Championship for women, losing on penalties to Sweden in 1984. Both legs of the final were televised live in Sweden; the tournament hardly merited a mention in the British press. But the women's game continued to grow apace, and by the early '90s over 300 clubs had registered with the WFA. There were around 9,000 players, but this compared poorly with the three-quarters of a million who played in Germany.

'Other countries have much more to offer at the moment,' laments Wheatley. 'The States has scholarships and they're already talking about setting up a professional league. They have a semi-professional set-up at the moment, as have Italy, Sweden and Norway. We had a player called Kelly Smith who was with us for two years – she was probably the best player in England. An American college watched her, liked what they saw and offered her a scholarship, so off she went. Our loss is definitely their gain. I can't blame Kelly, though. I'd have definitely done the same thing if those opportunities had been around when I was 18 or 19.

'Ted Copeland, who was the England women's manager until recently, is setting up his own college in East Durham where girls will train as much as they study, but given the choice between the bright lights of the States and East Durham, where would you go . . .?'

Predictably, in the light of their less-developed women's football system, England have yet to make a huge impact on the international game. Now managed by Hope Powell, a former Millwall Lionesses player and the first woman ever to take charge of an England team, the squad rarely see much success against their Continental rivals. Wheatley is optimistic, however.

'In ten or fifteen years' time, the whole standard of women's football in this country will have improved, which will have a positive effect on the England team. Two years ago we started an England Under-16 team which will educate the girls about nutrition and fitness and so on. The FA want to scout at the Centres of Excellence, drawing out the best players from them. The drawback is that clubs who don't have their own centre will be reluctant to send players to one based elsewhere. They'll be frightened of losing that player to another club. So teams like Watford or Mill Hill who have very good youth teams but no Centre of Excellence are reluctant to release their best girls. This means that they could miss out, because the Centres of Excellence should in theory be just that, and that's where the FA will be looking for the best players.'

Despite missing out on the treble for the second successive year in identical circumstances, Arsenal Ladies are still motivated and looking for fresh challenges. There is even talk of European competition. In fact, it's almost a reality.

'About a year ago there were big hopes for a European tournament for clubs, but the sponsors pulled out. There was a big meeting of women's associations at UEFA a while back, and things are in motion to establish a Champions' League-style competition, which could even come into effect as soon as next season.

'I'm not sure whether English clubs would be able to participate, though. Travelling would be a massive strain on finances and I don't know if we could afford it. The strongest backing comes from Germany, Norway and Holland, where the women's game is particularly strong, so I think it will happen in some form, it's just a question of whether we'll be involved or not.'

If and when this happens, Arsenal will be at the forefront of any English contribution. The English women's game still has a long way to go to catch up with its counterparts on the Continent and in the US, but with schemes such as the Centres of Excellence, and women like Clare Wheatley striving to ensure that women of the future have opportunities denied to present generations, it might not be too many years before England dominates the world scene. Then, perhaps, Ron Atkinson might care to rescind his remarks that 'women should be seen in the kitchen, the discotheque and the boutique, but certainly not in football'.

I left Highbury in good spirits. At last it looks like the women's game is breaking free from its undeserved jokey image and the Julie Ferretts of today won't have to put up with the laughter and lewd comments that dogged their predecessors. The standards are improving and the big clubs are getting behind the game. Maybe, just maybe, the worm is turning. But on my way back to the Arsenal tube I see a poster advertising men's clothing with the slogan 'Topless women's teams – now that's fantasy football!' – and I realise there's still a hell of a long way to go.

Leading the Cheers

Hendon v. Notts County, FA Cup First Round

When a non-league club is drawn against league opposition in the FA Cup, the first thing the media does is draw up a list of the daytime occupations of the part-timers. No preview or match report would be complete without commencing, 'The postmen, lorry drivers and teachers of [insert team here] took on . . .' They are usually a 'motley crew' or a 'ragtag assortment'. I think it's part of the TV deal which states that every non-league side featured in the FA Cup is contractually obliged to contain at least one of each of the following: milkman (to 'deliver the goods on Saturday'), postman (ditto), teacher ('who hopes to be chalking up the goals on Saturday'), window cleaner ('who'll be doing the rounds of the opposition defence') and someone who works in an office who can be interviewed wearing a shirt and tie, perched on the edge of a desk with a computer in the background.

Emphasis is placed on how the non-league footballer plays for the love of the game rather than financial recompense. But the non-league footballer can actually be a pretty shrewd operator. Why go into the professional game, trawling around the lower divisions on yearly contracts, not knowing if you'll be re-engaged the following season, and come out of the game at 34 ill-equipped to do anything else? Why risk the welfare of your family when you can hold down a steady job with a future and earn extra cash playing football in your spare time?

The standard of non-league football is often frowned upon, or even sniggered at, by pundits and fans of bigger clubs. Yet at the top end of the non-league game, the standard of football is easily equivalent to that of the Third Division, and often the Second Division, of the Football League. In terms of skill there is little to choose between them. What separates the semi-professional and the Football League sides is, more or less, fitness.

As a nimble 18-year-old I turned out a couple of times for the reserve side of a club in what is now the Ryman Premier Division. Now I would never make any claims to possess football ability, but I was way out of my depth. The speed of reaction, the pace of the game and the level of technique was far beyond that of even a good-standard Sunday team, and this was regarded as one of the poorest reserve teams the club had fielded in many years (which, coupled with an injury crisis and a number of internal ructions at the club was the reason I found myself pulling on a shirt for a couple of weeks). The standard was deemed to be so poor that the manager of the first team rarely allowed his players to turn out for the 'stiffs'. Yet it was miles above anything I had ever experienced in my admittedly limited and brief football career.

It was 'banker Paul Whitmarsh' who therefore posed the biggest threat to Notts County's cup hopes on this freezing Sunday lunchtime (and, heh heh, hoped to 'open his account' in the competition proper). What he does when not turning out for the Ryman Premier side at the weekend is of no concern. He is a Hendon footballer and today that's all we need to know. He could be the Bulgarian military attaché or a Colombian cocaine baron for all Hendon fans care. When he's bearing down on the goalkeeper in a one-on-one, all that matters is that he's capable of sticking the ball in the back of the net. Which on this occasion he isn't.

Are we told, for example, that he is up against the 'golfers, video-games enthusiasts, card players and nightclubbers' of Notts County? We see footballers for just under two hours every week, four if there's a midweek game, and that's all we're there for, to see them play football. Paul Whitmarsh is a footballer, so are his opponents today, so are Zinedine Zidane and Dennis Bergkamp. Okay, they might have made a better fist of the chance squandered by the Hendon striker in the opening minutes, but Paul Whitmarsh is Hendon's leading goalscorer. End of story. On this day, by what means he earns his living is not important.

I was searching for the elusive magic of the FA Cup, and today's match should have had all the right ingredients. Hendon, chugging along in the middle of the Ryman League Premier Division in front of crowds rarely topping the 300 mark, against Notts County, the country's oldest professional club, founder members of the Football League and cup winners themselves over a century ago. Having walked the Third Division the previous season, County are one of the biggest teams in the first round. Hendon, one of the great names of amateur football (their fanzine is called *The Sleeping Giant*), have a good record in the FA Cup. The previous season the Cricklewood side had gone to Brisbane Road in

ABOVE: Hugh Vivian, Amhara
District, Bahir Dar, Ethiopia,
November 1998

RIGHT: Hugh Vivian, North
London Olympians, Hackney,
August 1998

Cup fever, Leyton Pennant v Wembley

Clouds gather over Wembley's hopes of reaching their
spiritual home, FA Cup preliminary round

Clapton keeper Dean Mann regales the defence with his fishing stories

Meanwhile, Tilbury's Jamie Orman contemplates defeat just twelve
games away from the twin towers. Behind him, the Clapton
Barmy Army can barely conceal their delight

Football's merchandise revolution reaches Harrow Borough

Desperate defending for Thamesmead Town at Harrow Borough's Earlsmead, FA Cup second qualifying round

Clare Wheatley (centre), Arsenal and England, goes for goal

Bored with endlessly putting the ball in the net, Arsenal Ladies
resort to punting opposition players goalward instead

TOP: Hendon's cheerleaders desperately try to keep their circulation going in sub-zero temperatures, whilst Monty the Lamb frightens the children
INSET: The bright lights of the FA Cup come to Cricklewood
BOTTOM: Hendon v Notts County, coming to a back garden near you

Ken Chapman, anti-racist committee co-ordinator and
security adviser at Millwall. Cushy jobs, or what?

All white on the night at the New Den. Ken Chapman hopes the
phrase 'black and blue' will have new connotations for the Lions

Weed shall not be moved: Tooting & Mitcham United's
Sandy Lane, looking towards the Bog End

London fields, Hackney Marshes, 1999

the first round and beaten Orient 1–0 in a replay before going out 3–1 at Cardiff City.

The game had been switched to a Sunday lunchtime and made all-ticket. The logic behind this remains a mystery, as in the event the ground was only half-full. Outside the ground before the match, I saw an old man at the door of the club office. A steward was telling him that without a ticket he wasn't going to see the game. He looked like he'd been a fan for years (he had a green-and-white scarf around his neck; Hendon changed their colours to blue and white some years ago), the sort who would turn up week in, week out in all weathers. He'd seen the greatest amateur players of the golden age turn out on that pitch, but today, the occasion of the club's biggest game of the season, despite the fact that twice as many people who had bought tickets could have been comfortably accommodated, he wasn't going to see the match. And I was. Someone with just a fleeting interest in the fortunes of Hendon FC (although I had seen Iain Dowie playing for them a decade earlier, a face you tend not to forget). Presumably the switch and the all-ticket stipulation had been made by the police, thus depriving Hendon of some valuable income and depriving at least one veteran fan of the chance of seeing his team repeat the scare they gave another club who play in black and white, Newcastle United, in 1974 when Hendon drew 1–1 at St James's Park before going out in a replay.

The Claremont Road stadium is attached to the nearby Clitterhouse Park. Presumably the club chose not to adopt the Clitterhouse moniker on the grounds that with that name most blokes wouldn't know where to find it. And if they did they wouldn't know what to do when they got there. The park stages a number of local matches and the raised terracing means that if Hendon's match is uninspiring, solace can be found by turning your back on the game and watching a more interesting one over the fence.

The ground has seen some notable triumphs over the years, Hendon having clinched a number of Athenian and Isthmian League Champion-ships, and is well appointed, if a little aged. The main stand runs almost the length of the pitch, with covered terracing opposite and raised terracing behind both goals. Apart from the fact that today it is barely half-full, the atmosphere is old-fashioned and boisterous.

It is almost a living museum to ancient supporters' fads. There are inflatable bananas and bobble hats, someone's made a banner with 'Hendon for the Cup' written on it, and being waved from the covered terracing is the cardboard cut-out of the FA Cup wrapped in tin foil that was obligatory until recently. There are people here with flasks of tea, eight-foot-long bar-scarves and rosettes. The show-off-of-the-day award goes to the bloke near me sporting a bright-red 'Bedlington Terriers – FA Cup' baseball cap. The previous day the Terriers murdered Colchester 4–1, and the whiskery individual peering through milk-bottle specs at his programme has to let everyone know that he was there. An obvious groundhopper, he is swigging one of those synthetic milkshakes that only late-night garages sell, inserting fistfuls of Wheat Crunchies into his mouth and wearing enough man-made fibres to power the floodlights from static energy alone.

As he was present at the greatest giant-killing of the round, I give him grudging respect, even if the hat does look silly and will never be worn again. Rather like those jester-style hats that appear at cup finals and music festivals. Having been carried along by the festive atmosphere into buying these multi-coloured abominations, at which Dr Seuss would have baulked before planting one on the head of his famous cat, regretful punters presumably all discard the hats within 24 hours of purchase, wishing they could give them back. Next summer you'll probably find me at Glastonbury running a stupid-hat hire stall; I'll make a fortune.

I have the standard FA Cup wag standing behind me. Revelling in an audience five times larger than usual, he shares with us such gems as 'Why didn't you put your first team out, County?' as Hendon pile on the early pressure and 'Why didn't you bring a goalie with you, County?' after keeper Darren Ward fumbles a shot behind for a corner. Goalie. There's a word you don't hear very often these days. That went out with the big woolly rollnecks they used to equip custodians with. Yes, today, for nostalgia junkies like me, all our Christmases have come at once.

I am brought up to date with a bang, however, when the Hendon mascot ambles on to the pitch and starts grooving awkwardly to 'Don't You Want Me Baby' by the Human League. The character out on the pitch is apparently Monty the Hendon Lamb (wouldn't 'Minty' have been more apposite?). Alarmingly, Monty is trailing a gaggle of reluctant-looking pubescent cheerleaders in miniskirts and skimpy tops. It is a November day and it is absolutely bloody freezing. Far from being entertained by these poor unfortunates, undoubtedly coerced from their regular weekly classes with a matronly woman with her hair in a bun with promises of a 'big break' and the chance of being spotted by the army of showbiz talent-spotters that frequents the non-league game, I am tempted to rush on to the pitch with warm clothing and hot soup. What sort of harebrained fool came up with that idea? At least Monty the bloody Hendon Lamb is well insulated inside his costume; these poor girls are in line for hypothermia.

As they go through their routine, that irritating record by Cher where her voice goes all funny is all but drowned out by their teeth chattering. Presumably the demented marketing person responsible sees the fact that their lips are going a vibrant shade of Hendon blue as great for the club's corporate image. When the teams emerge into the Arctic tundra that Cricklewood has now become, the girls waggle their pom-poms and leave the pitch, presumably, so I think, to a well-heated changing-room for cupcakes and Bovril. A few minutes into the game, however, the beleaguered troupe are marched behind the goal like a line of bewildered ducklings, where they stand for the duration of the game. It is so cold that I give up taking notes by half-time, my fingers having been so numbed that I would have done better sticking the pen in my mouth and trying to write that way. But no, there they stand, being prodded by a nearby psychopath into the occasional routine. People have gone to prison for less.

The irrefutable proof that Hendon have invested in a second-hand copy of some ancient 'sports marketing: American style' booklet comes with the net containing blue-and-white balloons in the middle of the pitch. Unfortunately they'd skipped the paragraph which says you have to fill them with helium, so when the net is removed, the balloons bobble awkwardly across the pitch and nestle against the advertising hoardings.

The first half is the closest I have seen to the mythical 'good old-fashioned cup tie' all season. Hendon dominate, with Whitmarsh a constant threat to the panicky County defence. The home side create plenty of chances, looking very confident going forward (I suppose you would if your two strikers had banged in 27 goals in 20 games between them). Whitmarsh's early miss, however, when he puts the ball straight into Ward's arms when clean through, is the best chance of the game, followed closely by his curling shot shortly afterwards which hits the post. It's a pulsating first half, at the end of which Hendon receive a deserved ovation. They should be at least one goal up, however. County are all over the place at the back, much to the consternation of their couple of hundred fans segregated at one end of the ground.

The second half is grim. County look a little livelier, but one senses that Hendon's chance of winning the game vanished with the half-time whistle. The County defence, which galumphed around crashing into each other for the first 45 minutes, is behaving more as it should rather than like contestants on *It's a Knockout*. The game dies a death and the temperature drops further and further. I don't think I've ever been so cold at a football match.

The referee brings the match to a close, to the relief of everyone in the ground. The cheerleaders, now frozen completely solid, are wheeled away on barrows one by one to be thawed out with hairdryers.

County know they've had a let off. Once the second half began it was clear that the home side had run out of ideas, and the visitors were content to play out the remaining minutes and turn them over at Meadow Lane in the replay. Which they did, 3–0. At last, however, I had seen something of what made the cup such a highly regarded event.

Hendon is barely five miles from Wembley Stadium, but this match was a world away from the final. The competition proper is under way; Hendon's run lasts another 90 minutes. Never mind, their dream of reaching Wembley is still alive: one week later they entertain Rothwell Town in the FA Trophy. Hopefully, the services of the cheerleaders won't be called upon again. I fear, though, that we haven't seen the last of Monty the Hendon Lamb in Cricklewood . . .

MC Hammer

Jeremy Nicholas in the Worst Seat in the House

Now that football has become as showbiz as a round of golf with Bruce Forsyth, no aspect of the game has escaped the scrutiny of the shadowy marketing people. It is these anonymous figures who decide on such improvements to the atmosphere as stings of music when a goal is scored, big spongy hands for the kids and names on the backs of shirts. This last 'improvement' was allegedly to fall in line with 'the Continent', but can anyone remember where exactly in mainland Europe anyone had their names on the backs of their shirts before Britain? Because I certainly can't. Maybe I'm thinking of the wrong continent. Maybe the Antarctic league has been doing this for years. After all, how would they identify Captain Oates unless he had a skipper's armband on and his name across the back of his sealskin coat?

As those of us who watched the beautiful game before it was trendy look back with dewy-eyed nostalgia at the bad old days of crumbling terracing, fences and running the gauntlet of a comprehensive twatting for walking to the ground on the wrong side of the road, we do recall that one common complaint was the inaudibility of the tannoy at most grounds. Huge speaker horns would hang from the roof like the blunderbusses wielded by Yosemite Sam, but instead of unleashing volleys of grapeshot, the horns would instead emit a curious honking sound which someone would eventually identify as the team changes. Given the unintelligible parps and grunts that came from some clubs' systems, I'm sure that at least two Second Division clubs in the early '80s employed walruses as their announcers. Maybe it was the same walrus. Maybe he was freelance.

The pre-match music would consist of one LP of marching-band music and, inevitably, 'When You're in Love with a Beautiful Woman' by Dr Hook. As you perused your programme, there would be a sudden horrendous tearing noise as the needle was scraped across the vinyl just as the good doctor was getting into his stride. The announcer would then proceed to test the microphone by thumping it five times, thus frazzling any remaining life in the ancient speakers. A rustle of paper would be heard, a bit of coughing, and then the team changes would appear courtesy of a voice so fuzzy, boomy and inaudible that the microphone must have been inserted into some part of the announcer's anatomy.

Those days are long gone, however. Huge monitor speakers now hang from gantries on fearsome-looking chains or point at the stands from the side of the pitch, speakers which last saw service on stage in front of Aerosmith. The latest chart hits pound into your chest before 'We Will Rock You' transports you into a frenzy of anticipation as the teams assemble in the tunnel. Or not. Gone is the bumbling old duffer who would shuffle into a cupboard in the depths of the stadium and murmur into his ancient microphone, one of those enormous things the size of a shoe with the letters 'BBC' stuck on the top. Birthdays would be read out two weeks late, whilst the opposition names, when you could hear them, would be spectacularly mispronounced (for Charlton, Anthony Barness would frequently mutate into somebody called Tony Barnes).

Nowadays clubs look to professional broadcasters to provide the pre-, during- and post-match entertainment. Now that most people within a three-mile radius of the stadium can hear every nuance of every syllable thanks to the latest tweeters and bass bins audio technology can provide, the bumbling old duffer has been replaced by people who actually seem to know what they're doing. West Ham United can boast one such pro, the television and radio presenter Jeremy Nicholas.

Probably best known to those resident in the capital for his work at GLR, the BBC station for London, where he currently co-hosts the breakfast show, Nicholas has also anchored sports shows for Channel 5. Hailing from Redbridge, east London, he is a lifelong West Ham fan who, until he took over as the Hammers' MC, had been a season-ticket holder for a number of years.

After gaining a degree in engineering, Nicholas went on to earn a postgraduate qualification in journalism before joining Viking Radio in Hull and then moving on to BBC Radio Nottingham's sports desk. He stayed there for three years before becoming disillusioned with football after being present at the Hillsborough disaster and moving to London and the GLR news department. Since then, Nicholas has also carved out a career in television, anchoring some of Channel 5's European football coverage and the *Turnstile* and *Live and Dangerous* programmes. When the channel covered the Poland v. England match as its first major live sporting event, Nicholas was initially delighted to be asked to be part of the team, along with Brough Scott, Dominik Diamond and former glamour model Gail McKenna.

'I knew there was something wrong when I found out that they'd given Les Ferdinand and Alan Mullery to Gail McKenna to interview,' says Nicholas. 'I ended up with Jo Guest and the Cambridge United Moose. That's when I realised that there was something wrong with the priorities there . . .'

I first meet Nicholas in the studios of GLR in London's Marylebone High Street. With the classic timing that I have slowly been perfecting, I've arrived on a bad day. There's a tube strike and most of the scheduled guests haven't shown up. The last half-hour of the show sees Nicholas and co-presenter Claire McDonnell frantically scanning the newspapers for titbits to fill the airtime. Long records are hunted down and played. After the show Nicholas and McDonnell disappear for 20 minutes before Nicholas emerges looking irritated. 'Sorry about that,' he says. 'We had to have a bit of a "clear the air" meeting about this morning's fiasco.'

As we sit and talk in a coffee shop over the road from the radio station and the conversation turns to football, Nicholas relaxes a bit. Whilst not as chirpy as he is on radio and television, it's clear that West Ham is a major part of his life (whenever someone mentions the Hammers or one of their players on his radio programme, he immediately breaks out into applause). I ask him how he came to be the matchday announcer at Upton Park.

'Basically what happened is that I wrote to the club when I renewed my season ticket asking if I could move forward from my previous seat. There's a rite of passage in the West Stand at Upton Park: as the old fans die off, the people behind move forward. It's a kind of pecking order. I'd managed to get as far as row F, and I'm only in my thirties, so I was quite proud of myself.

'Anyway, I'd used my headed notepaper which describes me as a broadcaster. A few days later I received a phone call from the club saying that they were thinking of changing the announcer at Upton Park, they'd heard of me and knew what I could do, and they wondered if I'd be interested. The problem was that I'd got as far as row F and wasn't sure if I could give that up! Also the tannoy system was so awful that no one could hear it. I honestly couldn't pass opinion on my predecessor because I'd never really heard him, that's how bad it was. So I said no, but agreed to call in at the club for a chat.

'After that, I had the same dream for three nights running. I dreamt that England had won the World Cup and I was out on the pitch interviewing Rio Ferdinand, introducing him to the crowd. So when I woke up from the dream the third time, I thought, actually, I really fancy doing that. So I rang the club and that's how it all started.'

His post-World Cup tannoy debut, however, was memorable for different reasons. Rather than congratulating the Hammers' defender on winning the World Cup, Nicholas found himself caught in the cauldron which awaited the arrival of the man identified most with torpedoing England's chances in France. West Ham's first home match of the 1998–99 season was against Manchester United, David Beckham's first match away from Old Trafford since his sending-off against Argentina earlier in the summer. Anti-Beckham fever had swept across the country – a mannequin clad in a Beckham England shirt and a sarong had been hung by the neck outside one pub. Obviously, a warm, understanding welcome was the last thing that would await him at Upton Park.

Beckham's predicament was worsened by the fact that he's an east London boy, born and raised in Leytonstone. The fact he joined Manchester United was seen by many Hammers fans as some kind of betrayal, even though, as Nicholas points out, Beckham and his family are all confirmed fans of the red menace and the young prodigy never wanted to play for anyone else.

'It was quite a daunting occasion for my first appearance behind the microphone,' says Nicholas. 'Being a Channel 5 presenter, I'm used to small audiences, so 26,000 people was quite a big gig. The police held a couple of briefings and they called the fanzines together and said look, ease off. Even so, when I read out the teams before the game and got to number seven, David Beckham, there was the most horrendous hostile booing. It was a weird experience all round, because when you do TV and radio there's no audience, no feedback about what you're saying. I'd done a few corporate things before, but nothing like this. It was all pretty daunting. In the end, though, it all went off fairly peacefully. I think the club was just happy there hadn't been a riot.

'After the game I read out the other scores from the Premiership. I think it's good to make the odd comment about who's won or lost, particularly teams that are your rivals. It usually raises a cheer or a laugh. On this day, Spurs had lost, so before I gave the score I said, "You'll like this . . ." Apparently, up in the directors' box Bobby Charlton turned round and said, "He shouldn't do that, he shouldn't say that sort of thing." When the club told me, I said, "To be honest, I don't care. I spend all week on the BBC being unbiased so it's nice to be a little bit subjective – it's what football is all about. I'm a West Ham fan, as are most of the 26,000 other people in the ground. Of course we're happy when Spurs lose."'

After our chat in Marylebone, Nicholas invites me along to West Ham's Premiership match with Newcastle United to watch him in action. Due to the location of his cubbyhole at Upton Park, there's little else to see anyway, positioned as it is low down by a corner flag with a pillar obstructing most of the view.

'I turned up for the Manchester United game all excited about the season. We've got some good players and, as usual, we were optimistic about the coming season. We'd won up at Sheffield Wednesday the week before, with Ian Wright scoring, so I was thinking we could win a cup this season, and probably qualify for Europe as well. And then I came in here and thought, hang on, I'm not going to see a bloody thing. There are some seats behind the enclosure for the disabled near the box, and there was a policeman sitting in one. I said to him, "Look, I've got to sit here." So there I was, sitting in the crowd with my microphone.'

On arriving in the box around an hour and a half before kick-off, Nicholas goes through some of the requests and messages. 'This is the sort of thing I get,' he says, pushing a fax towards me. On the same day, England play Scotland in the Five Nations tournament. The fax has come from a group of people who are taping the game and asking Nicholas not to give out the score. 'Well, 26,000 other people are dying to know the score, so I think we can safely ignore that one,' he says.

'During the game you get some stupid messages phoned through from reception. It's amazing how many women go into labour during West Ham's home games. I mean, there are probably only 10,000 people in the ground of an age to have children, but every week there seems to be at least one wife or girlfriend going into labour. We must have the most fertile supporters in the country. Either that or there's something about the way we play that induces childbirth . . . We also get a ridiculous number of people who've got someone else's ticket for them and can't remember where to meet, and loads of cars parked in the wrong place.'

I am almost disappointed to find no LPs of marching-band music. Nor is there any sign of Dr Hook. There's not even a turntable. Instead, two CD players are stacked neatly, one on top of the other, in the corner, whilst in front of the announcer's chair is a mixing desk. Just one look at the fader, dials and buttons would have been enough to send the old-style announcer screaming from the box. Nicholas unpacks a pile of CDs from his rucksack and begins to choose his playlist for the afternoon.

'I get to choose what I play and am given £35 in HMV vouchers to spend for every match. The bloke who did this before me had a strange way of choosing stuff: he'd play Billy Bragg because he's from Barking. You know, "Here's one from a local lad," that sort of thing.

'I play a lot of modern stuff, but there's no point in playing real cutting-edge stuff because no one will know it here. Plus everyone's talking to their mates and reading their programme and stuff. I try to mix it all up a bit. I think people want well-known rocking stuff like Robbie Williams. I play a bit of the Spice Girls and All Saints for the Junior Hammers, but I refuse to play "We Are the Champions" because we aren't, and I don't think we will be in my lifetime. And yes, I will stick on "Simply the Best" and "We Will Rock You", because you hear them all the time anyway.

'I've tried to throw in some classical stuff before the teams come out, which works quite well. I've played Prokofiev's *Romeo and Juliet* because it's about two families coming together for a scrap which is a bit like football. Mussorgsky's *Night on the Bare Mountain* seemed to go down quite well, because it's quite stirring.

'The most important piece of music is "Bubbles", of course, which has to be played as the teams come out. In fact, you'll have to help me out here.'

Fortunately, given the less-than-ideal location of the box at West Ham, Jeremy Nicholas has a TV monitor linked to the big screen which is situated at the corner of the ground. My job today is to look at the screen, scrutinising the players' tunnel, and to shout as soon as the ref begins to lead the players on to the field. I'm not helped by the fact that the director keeps switching shots around the ground. Fortunately I manage to avoid the wrath of 26,000 Irons by spotting the movement at the right moment, so the 'play' button can be hit on cue.

Nicholas runs through the team changes, gees up the crowd some more and can then relax as the game kicks off. I ask him about West Ham's mixed season.

'We haven't really had a settled team at any time,' he opines. 'Harry keeps tinkering. We had all that business about the foreign players, the Boogers thing and everything, but Harry hasn't got a blank chequebook like a lot of Premiership managers. That's why we get the Croatians and the Romanians, because they're a lot cheaper. Slaven Bilic was a good buy, but he was too greedy. Dumitrescu was just awful, and I think Raduciouiu put him off overseas players for good. There was that famous occasion when he should have been reporting to the ground to set off for an away League Cup tie but instead was shopping at Harvey Nichols with his wife and mother.

'That was the last straw, really. After that he concentrated more on good, solid British lads like Lomas, Hartson and Kitson. The money we got from Everton for Bilic was safely in the bank, and those three players kept us up that season. We had players who could win the ball, which we hadn't seen here for a while.

'Then Hartson got all chubby. He'd scored loads of goals in the first half of the season and everyone said, blimey, he's good. But it was like a secret that only West Ham fans were in on: we could see he was unfit and his first touch had gone. He'd lost a lot of the fans' affection over the Berkovic business when he kicked the bloke in the head in front of the TV cameras. Kicking people in the head isn't really the West Ham way, especially when it's someone on your own team! It was a good bit of business on Harry's part to get £7 million out of Wimbledon for him.

'The important thing was to use the money quickly, because there were rumours flying around that we had to sell players to finance the building of a new stand. Fortunately he brought in Minto and Foe, who we keep hearing is the new Vieira but who hasn't really done anything yet. The Di Canio signing is working out well. I can't really take him seriously because he looks like he's playing in slippers, but he's going to have to do a lot to win over the fans here because we have quite high standards. Pushing the referee over is not something we approve of here.'

Nicholas is aware that West Ham have a long way to go before they can compete with the giants of the game. 'The fans here know that we can't afford to buy the top players. The only way we could get Di Canio was because he's damaged goods after the Alcock incident, a bit like a piece of porcelain with a chip in it. Like most fans, I thought "oh no" when we bought him, but then as soon as someone starts playing for you, you instantly like them, don't you?'

Half-time approaches, so Nicholas and his assistant, who also runs the Sunday football team Heart of North London, for whom the broadcaster turns out in Regent's Park, scan Teletext for the half-time scores. The half-time entertainment is provided by the Hammerettes dance troupe. Their choreographer masterminds the music in the box but is not happy when the camera crew beam pictures on to the big screen. As the girls go though their routine in skimpy T-shirts and shorts, it is not long before the director zooms in on one of their backsides. The screen in the corner is filled with a pert, wiggling, 20-foot-square arse. 'I've told them about that loads of times,' splutters the boss. 'They know they're not supposed to do that.'

The match itself has been uneventful. West Ham will go on to win 2–1 with two goals from Di Canio. Newcastle just don't look in the slightest bit interested. Alan Shearer produced a fine save from Shaka Hislop in the fourth minute, but then seemed to think that his work was done. He spent the rest of the match stomping around and sulking. The only international-quality characteristic he showed was some Olympic-standard whinging.

There had been moves to bring Lennox Lewis to the game for an interview with Nicholas on the pitch at half-time, but it evidently didn't come off. Instead Nicholas returns to the box having conducted a couple of competitions on the touchline.

'Van Hooijdonk had talks with West Ham when he left Celtic,' he says, warming to his theme again, 'but he chose Nottingham Forest because he said West Ham would be relegated. When it was announced that Forest had been relegated last season, there was a massive cheer here. We hate being seen as a middling club that players use as a stepping stone to go on to better things. We only want to see people who want to play for West Ham, not people who are just turning out until something better comes along.'

The fearsome reputation of the Hammers crowd has diminished in recent years. Paul Ince apart, ex-players are mostly given a good reception. 'Hugo Porfiro was given a great ovation here this season. When Tony Cottee scored for Leicester in front of the South Bank, everyone clapped. Even Jamie Redknapp gets a cheer as a kind of local boy made good. If West Ham played QPR, Iain Dowie would get a good reception. He was crap but he tried really hard, which we appreciate at Upton Park. But if you're photographed in a Manchester United shirt before you leave, or do what Bilic did and announce that you're going to Everton to "win things", you won't get much of a welcome down here.'

As the Irons cruise towards a comfortable victory, all Nicholas has to do is announce a couple of substitutions. This allows him more time to hold forth on his favourite subject. He is optimistic about the future at West Ham.

'When you've got players like Rio Ferdinand, Frank Lampard and Joe Cole on long contracts, it's fantastic for the future. You can tell that Cole is a class player, but he's got a lot to learn. At the moment he comes on as a substitute and just runs around like mad. The hard thing at this level is knowing where to be at the right time. Give him a year and they'll be moulding the team around him. He's already a bit special: in training five-a-sides they apparently give the other team a five-goal start. The thing is not to put too much pressure on him. Is he the Messiah, or is he a Brian? You know, "He's not the Messiah, he's just an ordinary run-of-the-mill midfielder." It could all get very Monty Python; we could all be running around shouting about the "miracle of Joe's shoe". Twelve clubs tried to poach him, big clubs were offering him lots of incentives to leave West Ham, but he's chosen to stay.

'There isn't much loyalty left in football, but I don't think you can really blame people in the end. Players want to play at the highest level, in Europe and so on, and until we play at a ground that can hold more than 26,000 people we're not going to be able to compete. We're planning to rebuild the East and West Stands to increase the capacity. The West Stand doesn't even run the length of the pitch because there's a school next door (the playground becomes the players' car park on matchdays), so the club are going to knock the school down and pay for it to be relocated. That will take the capacity up to 36,000. An extra 10,000 people at, say, 25 quid a head is a lot of extra money to spend on big-name players.'

The final whistle brings to a close a largely uninspiring match but one which propels West Ham into eighth position. The possibility of European football remains. Nicholas relays the final scores to the departing fans and lets the music run whilst he packs away.

We walk around the perimeter of the pitch in front of an empty stadium. 'I like it when it's like this,' says Nicholas. 'To think that half an hour ago there were 26,000 people screaming and shouting, and now it's totally empty.' Joe Cole is doing a little light training at one end of the field. The groundstaff are busily replacing divots into one of the country's best pitches. As we cut a corner, passing just behind the corner flag but not actually stepping on to the pitch, one of the groundsmen yells at us to keep to the track. This clearly irritates Nicholas; earlier in the season the groundsman had refused him permission to walk on to the pitch before the game just to have his photograph taken for a magazine feature. He walks across the hallowed turf towards the forking groundsman, pretending not to hear.

It's not the most exciting job in the world, being a matchday announcer. But as football becomes increasingly commercial, the job becomes much more sanitised. The rivalry and bias that helped to make football the huge cash cow that it has become is all too often played down. Neutrality appears to be the game's watchword these days, a fake 'may the best team win' for the benefit of neutrals watching matches from their armchairs. Jeremy Nicholas is a real fan. Fair play to the Hammers for giving him the job. As long as his enthusiasm and bias can be conveyed to like-minded souls over the Upton Park PA, there's hope for football.

The Holligan Element

Leyton Orient v. Kingstonian, FA Cup Second Round

Mark Warren ran the line at the 1998 World Cup final in Paris. Five months before this FA Cup second-round tie in east London, it was his sharp eyes that had scanned the back line looking for Ronaldo's or Zidane's appearance behind the defence before the ball was kicked. He may have anticipated a slightly easier evening when he arrived at Leyton Orient's three-sided ground to referee a match in front of just over 3,000 people between a mid-table Third Division side and their opponents, a bunch of part-timers from suburban Surrey. If he expected an easy time, however, he was sadly mistaken, as this game exploded in the final few minutes.

Kingstonian and Orient had fought out an uninspiring second-round tie at the K's architecturally bland Kingsmeadow ground on a bright but chilly Sunday morning ten days earlier. Despite a late flurry of attacks by the Conference side, Orient's goalkeeper Chris MacKenzie had pulled off a couple of important saves to keep the O's in the competition.

Orient might have approached the replay with a little less relish than many clubs in their position, for in each of the previous two seasons they had been beaten at home in the FA Cup by non-league opposition. The previous year, Hendon had won 1–0 following a 2–2 draw at Claremont Road, scoring with their only chance of the whole game, whilst in the 1996–97 competition it was Stevenage Borough who had done the damage.

Both sides went into this game in good form. Orient's run of ten games unbeaten had been ended by Peterborough United the previous Saturday, a stretch which had taken the O's up to sixth in the table. Kingstonian were unbeaten in 11 matches in the Conference and were managed by Geoff Chapple, the man who had guided Woking to their famous FA Cup and FA Trophy exploits over the previous decade. A pre-season friendly had ended 2–1 to the K's a few months earlier. All the ingredients were in place for a good game.

The match had the potential to be a tale of two strikers. Orient fielded a French international, 36-year-old Amara Simba, up front, whilst Kingstonian included young forward Gavin Holligan, exactly half Simba's age, who was playing potentially his last game for the club.

Born in Senegal, Simba moved to France as a youth. Gerard Houllier spotted him playing amateur football and signed him for Paris St Germain in 1986. Seven years, three international caps and three French 'Goal of the Season' awards later, the lanky striker moved on to Monaco, then managed by Arsène Wenger. A spell in Mexico followed, before Simba eventually rolled up at Brisbane Road early in 1998. He became an instant hero to the O's faithful. Holligan, meanwhile, began 1998 at the lowly non-league club Walton and Hersham. He joined Kingstonian at the start of the 1998–99 season and immediately attracted the attention of West Ham United. Harry Redknapp agreed a £150,000 deal. Holligan, however, would not join the Hammers until Kingstonian's interest in the FA Cup had come to an end.

As I took up my position near the halfway line in the paddock in front of the main stand, I looked round to find a scary sight. There sat Harry Redknapp, keeping an eye on his protégé, flanked by Frank Lampard and, curiously, John Wark. Lampard is a terrifying-looking bloke with his flowing dark hair, piercing stare and formidable facial hair. John Wark looks equally intimidating, like Lampard steely of gaze, dark of hair and with that manicured bandito moustache. All three were dressed in matching black overcoats. Redknapp looked like a galactic emperor flanked by his warlords. I looked away before I was caught by the Lampard gaze and zapped by laser beams from the hairy one's eyes.

These days Brisbane Road is a three-sided affair. I suspected that the gap behind the goal where a big bank of terracing used to be had been caused by the carnage following the arrival of Lampard, Wark and Redknapp's mother ship, but it turned out that two years earlier the club, in its wisdom, had decided to knock down the south terracing without actually ensuring that there were sufficient funds to replace it. Hence three rows of advertising hoardings are pushed right up behind the goal where the away end used to be. In the distance, the lights of Canary Wharf can be seen illuminating the night sky where the South Stand should be.

The removal of the south terrace also necessitated the demolition of the two floodlight pylons at that end. They have been replaced with what appear to be two sets of lights filched from the car park of an out-of-town shopping centre. In each corner, two long, low-level rows of white lights illuminate the south end of the pitch. It's almost as if two of the Osmonds have been instructed to sit on a pole in the corner of the pitch and bare their pearlers.

The three-sided nature of the ground makes for a curious atmosphere. The Kingstonian fans are housed at the other end of the paddock to where I stand. They are just about invisible behind a high dividing wall. Opposite, over the halfway line is an illuminated sign informing spectators that they aren't at Brisbane Road after all but at something called the Matchroom Stadium. The legacy of Barry Hearn's ownership of the club is there for all to see in garish neon, lit up like the sign over a kebab shop. Early in his tenure, Hearn frequently brought along some of his snooker-playing cronies to wave to the crowd before kick-off. Thankfully that practice has stopped; their replacement by page-three girls also didn't last too long.

The home side took the field in their curious red-and-white checked shirts, whilst Kingstonian emerged in yellow shirts with light-blue shorts. Presumably Mark Warren was given a bit of a shock when he suddenly thought he was leading out Croatia and Brazil. One look around the sparsely populated, three-quarters-built stadium soon brought him smack up to date, however. It was nice to see that Kingstonian were reviving the tradition of having shirt numbers high up on the backs of their shirts, rather than just above the waistband, which appears to be the current trend. Presumably high shirt numbers died out with the advent of the Chris Waddle mullet hairstyle that became inexplicably popular with footballers during the late '80s. The current trend for short back and sides has meant that the shirt number can now gradually return to its former glories between the shoulder blades.

Whilst waiting for the kick-off I absorb some of the East End friendliness for which Orient is renowned. Groups of friends greet each other warmly, backs are slapped, runs to the tea bar made. An atmosphere of genuine *bonhomie* pervades the paddock, whilst a couple of drummers in the stand commence their attempts to whip the crowd into a frenzy in time for the kick-off.

There also appears to be some sort of celebrity lookalike convention gathering here behind the dugouts. Bianca from *Eastenders* is deep in discussion with Van Morrison in front of me (hopefully she was advising the rhythm'n'blues legend of his unfortunate choice of headgear: an Umbro bronx hat), whilst Caroline Quentin manoeuvres past me with two cheeseburgers in each hand, heading in the direction of Foghorn Leghorn. Okay, I made the last one up. I say I made the cotton-picking last one up.

Once the match starts, all the good feeling generated up to now flies off through the gap where the South Stand should be in the direction of Canary Wharf, and 90 minutes of abuse commences. Most of it comes from a bloke to my right who looks like he's stepped straight out of an Open University programme from the '70s. Sporting the thick National Health-style glasses that you surely can't get any more, and topped with an unruly mop of '70s hair, he hoots obscenities at the visiting players in a high-pitched voice throughout the entire game. It's an impressive performance – he even manages to consume a hamburger without interrupting the flow of invective. Most of it is pure, unadulterated abuse. The most inventive he gets is when a Kingstonian defender applauds a team-mate's clearance into touch to thwart a threatening Orient attack. 'Oh, you think that was good football do you, number five? Well, you must be a cunt then,' says our man, wittily.

For all his fighting talk, Mister Sweary couldn't punch his way out of a paper bag. But somehow, the low wall that separates this sad individual from the brick shithouse of a defender he has just labelled with the most offensive title it is possible to use without resorting to intricate sign language makes him untouchable. It's weird really. If Mister Sweary had started on K's Simon Stewart in a pub, he would have been taken into the car park and given a thorough and comprehensive twatting the likes of which he would never receive again. Yet Stewart has to pretend he hasn't heard. Amidst all the Cantona kung-fu controversy a few years back and the tide of condemnation, I couldn't prevent a little voice in my head saying 'Nice one, Eric'. I imagine professional footballers across the land allowed themselves a wry smile as Matthew Simmonds was thudded in the chest by the Frenchman's boots.

Much amusement is derived amongst the ranks from England's World Cup official's long legs, tight shorts and sticky-out bum. He runs like Penelope Pitstop. Faced with such promising material, though, Orient's relentless abuser fails to find anything remotely original to break up the unremitting flow of swearwords.

Early in the game I head for the tea bar behind the stand. As I wait for my hot dog, an ear-splitting roar that sounds like God shutting his fingers in his car door thunders through my head like Armageddon. Convinced that at the very least the stand is collapsing, I hurl myself to the floor and cover my head. When I venture a look out from beneath my elbow, the entire catering staff are leaning over the counter looking at me. One is holding out my hot dog. It turns out that the world isn't ending after all, Wim Waelschaerts has just put the O's in front. Whereas many clubs have now introduced a short musical sting to accompany goals in a pathetic attempt to make the game more showbiz, Orient play a recording of a man with a deep voice shouting 'Gooooooaaaallllll!!!'. About six feet above my head is a tannoy horn the size of a euphonium honking away with the news of the O's opener. I stand up. A recently discarded teabag has adhered itself to my knee.

I return to the action just in time to see Kingstonian's Eddie Akuamoah not only being stretchered off but being zipped into what appears to be a body bag. Perhaps the tannoy blast was too much for him as well.

The half-time whistle allows Mister Sweary a breather, presumably to think up some more swearwords and suck on a few throat lozenges. I don't know if it's a tradition at every ground with a paddock in front of the stand, but at half-time everyone around me turns 180 degrees and just stares at the people in the seats. Like when someone else yawns and you find yourself unable to prevent a jaw-cracking, mouth-splitting yawn of your own, I unconsciously do likewise. It must be a bit unnerving for the people sitting there, suddenly confronted with a sea of faces all looking at them for no apparent reason. There's not much to see apart from Messrs Redknapp, Lampard and Wark looking moody and mysterious. It does become clear, though, that Barry Hearn appears to have his own personal camera crew following him around. He is bathed in light while a cameraman squats in front of him, a big furry microphone hanging just above his head. Don't know what that was all about.

In the opening minutes of the second half, as the crowd in the paddock completes a full 360-degree turn to face the front again, Orient appear to have put the game beyond doubt with a marvellous flying header from Simba. The O's striker flew gracefully through the air to meet a right-wing cross and power it past Steve Farrelly in the Kingstonian goal. Not bad for a 36-year-old. The Orient faithful go bananas: Simba is a popular chap in this corner of east London.

The second goal prompts Geoff Chapple to bring on the boy wonder Gavin Holligan, whose first taste of football at professional level is a volley of abuse from barely ten yards away courtesy of our man with the meanest mouth in London. And this was when he was just waiting to come on.

Holligan turns the game, and looks like a shrewd buy for Harry Redknapp. Within minutes of his arrival, Orient's Chris MacKenzie fumbles a cross in the area and Holligan reacts like lightning to stab the ball into the net before anyone else could move. Shortly afterwards, his cheeky lob over MacKenzie into the top corner is controversially disallowed for offside. Orient have suddenly completely lost their way and are totally unable to cope with Holligan's pace and enthusiasm. The non-league side create chance after chance and are very unlucky not to draw level.

With about five minutes left on the clock, Farrelly comes hurtling out of his goal almost to the halfway line and clatters Matthew Joseph right by the touchline. Right in front of the most abusive man in Britain, who becomes so excited he actually takes off and floats above the ground for several minutes, apoplectic with rage. Farrelly has to go, but pandemonium breaks out. Players surround the referee, whilst Kingstonian's coach berates the linesman for his part in Farrelly receiving his marching orders. When the O's fans abuse him in turn, he runs immediately to a policeman and attempts to point out the culprits. Whenever the policeman looks in the direction of the alleged perpetrators, the K's coach rather uncharitably makes what can most politely be described as a representation of the male masturbatory act. Whenever the policeman looks back, the coach is suddenly doing something innocuous like scratching his head.

As Farrelly troops off towards the tunnel, I look towards Mister Sweary's spot to see his reaction. He isn't there, however. He's hanging over the tunnel pouring yet more invective over the unfortunate keeper. When a policeman starts showing an interest, suddenly he is back on his old spot whistling, his hands in his pockets, absent-mindedly toeing a pebble around his feet. He'd returned with a speed that defied the human eye. If it had been a cartoon, he'd have had a halo over his head.

The final minutes pass relatively uneventfully. Farrelly's dismissal has ended Kingstonian's hopes of retrieving the match, and Gavin Holligan is free to accept the West Ham shilling. Mark Warren has earned a police escort from the pitch, allowing Mister Sweary a final attempt at rupturing his own spleen.

The reward for Orient was a glamorous third-round tie away to Southport. Come the end of the season, both clubs would reach Wembley, but not in this competition. Orient earned a place in the Third Division play-off final, whilst Kingstonian earned Geoff Chapple the fourth FA Trophy success of his managerial career. Orient lost. Mister Sweary's reaction is unprintable.

The Supporters' Club

Peter Varney and the Rise of Charlton Athletic

If you could run your football club for a day, what would you do? Bring back terracing? Give your friends free season tickets? Play yourself up front because you couldn't do any worse than the pair you've got at the moment?

Imagine being put in charge of the club you've supported since you were Kevin Keegan's height. Saunter unchallenged among the corridors and offices that lurk mysteriously beneath the stand. Be on nodding terms with the players, take in the odd round of golf with the manager and captain. Fire the steward that gives you a hard time every time you stand up to watch a corner.

Very few people make the transition from the stands to the offices. Many chairmen profess lifelong support for their team, then can't tell you the year they won the FA Cup. Genuine fans on the board are a rarity. Charlton Athletic are fortunate to have an administration drawn almost entirely from the club's fanbase. Indeed, its communications manager and marketing chief were two of the most rebellious fans against the administration that sold the club out of The Valley in the mid-'80s.

The club's regeneration following its return to The Valley is fairytale enough for most supporters: from First Division also-rans in a three-sided ground to the Premiership in six years. But one fan suddenly found himself at the helm of this buoyant, throbbing vessel as it steamed towards the end of the century in better shape than ever, whilst fending off job offers from some of the biggest names in football.

I was a little bit late meeting Peter Varney, Charlton Athletic's managing director. Now that Greenwich is, apparently, the centre of the universe thanks to the construction within its environs of what appears to be a large, acupunctured boiled egg, all the surrounding streets have been dug up, widened, narrowed, repainted, diverted or just fenced off

121

to show that Greenwich means business and anyone who thinks they can drive around and park when and where they like can just piss off.

I waited in the foyer of The Valley's new glass fasciaed West Stand, a towering construction which dominates a stadium totally unrecognisable from the terraced cavern that stood there less than a decade earlier. The new West Stand illustrates the drive and ambition of the club's administration. I am sitting facing a glass cabinet containing the trophy Charlton received for their play-off victory over Sunderland at Wembley the previous May. Spotlights play on its polished silver veneer, red and white ribbons hang from its handles. Although receiving silverware for finishing fourth may seem a little incongruous to those teams that finished above them yet didn't have a nice money-spinning day out at Wembley, Charlton are the last to complain. The tenacity and determination shown by the team in that astonishing 4–4 draw at Wembley followed by the successful conversion of 13 consecutive penalties before Michael Gray scuffed his shot for the Wearsiders summed up the spirit that has pervaded Charlton Athletic from the boardroom downwards since the late '80s.

Okay, I'm biased. I've been a Charlton supporter since I was a nipper and I'm immensely proud of how far the club has come since plumbing the depths of its existence not so very long ago. When Peter Varney arrived and led me up to the Millennium Suite at the very top of the stand, overlooking the stadium, I gave him probably the easiest ride he'll ever have from an interviewer. Whilst I managed to restrain myself from leaping over the table and throwing my arms around him in thanks for the club's progress, my questioning stopped only just short of 'Everything's lovely here, isn't it?'.

Charlton are a busy club these days. Varney's original intention had been to use the boardroom for our interview, but on bursting through the door we found ourselves interrupting a corporate seminar by one of the many businesses that hire The Valley's facilities. Eventually we settle for a place up in the gods, overlooking the pitch from a great height at the top of the West Stand.

Varney exudes an air of affable impatience. He is friendly and likeable, yet obviously in possession of a strong businesslike drive. A supporter since the early '60s when his father used to bring him to matches, Varney first became actively involved with the club through his work as a director of the British Brain and Spine Foundation. He helped the Addicks' veteran Steve Gritt with fund-raising events for one of his children and was asked by the Charlton chairman Richard Murray to become involved on the commercial side of the club's activities.

'I wasn't sure at first, because Charlton was always my hobby. It's a bit different moving from that to being responsible for running the business of the club. It wasn't an instantaneous "yes" on my part; I thought about it for a couple of months before agreeing to take over the commercial side. Shortly after I did so, the chairman and I agreed that I should become managing director and oversee the day-to-day running of the club, releasing the chairman to look after his side of things more.'

It has been hard for Varney to make the transition from supporter to administrator. 'I'd be lying if I didn't say I don't enjoy the home games as much as I used to,' he says. 'When you're a fan, you have a certain routine, don't you? I'd leave home at the same time, take the same route, stop off for fish and chips, pick my mate up, go in the Covered End behind the goal – there's no pressure like there is when you become heavily involved. You're much more relaxed as a fan, and free to abuse the manager and abuse the team, which everyone does.

'When you're involved, suddenly things become very different. If I was to go out of the door at the back of the stand on a matchday, I wouldn't be able to walk 50 yards without people stopping me and wanting to talk about one issue or another. It's also different in other ways, because you know what the financial effect will be on the club if they don't win. Matchdays are definitely not as enjoyable as they were.'

Varney arrived at the club towards the end of 1997, before Charlton's march to Wembley and the Premiership promised land.

'When I came in we'd been in the First Division for a while, but there was a great deal of hard work going on behind the scenes. The things that happened since my arrival have been the reward for all that endeavour.

'We had a share issue which raised the money to go out and buy Eddie Youds and Danny Mills, who underpinned the great run we had at the end of the promotion season and ultimately the match at Wembley. After that we had the increased season-ticket sales and this £7 million stand where we're sitting. The club is a completely different one from what it was even just a year ago. I like to think also that we're putting out a different image within the football world itself. I think previously we had this image of "little Charlton", with huts and portakabins every-where, but I think now we're more accepted as a serious football club.'

As part of Charlton's transition, the business and commercial side of the club has developed beyond recognition in the past few years. Whilst those at the helm today are all fans of one sort or another, they are business people first, a necessity of the modern game. It also means more work for the managing director.

'I was talking to my counterpart at Leicester about this and he found the same thing was true. We're a PLC now, and what tends to happen is that you have the PLC, which is the master, and the football club, which is a subsidiary of the PLC. The PLC has a lot of demands on time – you have to produce interim results, annual reports, there are share issues and all sorts of things which are PLC activities. But really there's just one management, so lots of those facets of running a football club are answerable to the PLC and the shareholders. Bear in mind that the shareholders aren't only the supporters but also the city, private investors, which means that the nature of the work I do is quite varied. One day I might be dealing with a £3 million share issue, which we had a few months back, and then receive a call to come down to reception because there's a guy who insists on seeing the managing director because his burger was cold the previous Saturday.

'Because I'm a long-term fan – my father first brought me down here in 1960 – I think it's very important that if someone wants to complain about something to the managing director then I should respond. I don't fob it off on somebody else. So in fact I probably cause myself problems that I shouldn't necessarily have. People know I'm a fan, and in fact a lot of them still call me 'Reg', which is a nickname I've had for a long time for obvious reasons. I think people probably see me as more approach-able than the normal football-club managing director. I also write a page in the programme where I do my best to tell it like it is. We do have a definite commitment to being open here. A lot of clubs seem to have the attitude that what they use their money for is nothing to do with the fans. But I believe that most people are intelligent enough to understand why you're making the decisions that you're making, whereas I think in the past things followed the same pattern: the team's playing badly, so sack the manager. If things still don't get any better then sack the board. If that doesn't work then I don't know what happens. But one of the reasons that happens is that among chairmen – and I think this is mainly true of the lower divisions – there is a belief that you don't communicate what is regarded as privileged information. We don't believe in that here.'

Charlton were one of the first clubs to have a supporter on the board elected by and accountable to the supporters. The current incumbent, Mick Gebbett, can be found on matchdays banging a big drum behind the goal to help stoke up the atmosphere.

'There are no other meetings when he's not there, I can tell you that. We don't all go round the corner when he's gone and have another meeting or anything like that: he takes part in all the decision-making.'

This is all a far cry from the summer of 1985, when a group of directors took the decision that Charlton would leave The Valley to share Selhurst Park with Crystal Palace. At the time, Greenwich Council had a representative on the board of directors who was kept totally in the dark about the move. The first he knew of it was at the same time as the supporters, when he walked into the ground for a home match with Crystal Palace and had a leaflet pushed into his hand announcing that the club was on the move.

'We're very keen that the supporters have a say in things, be it season-ticket prices or whatever. The fans should have a say in how the club is run. It's important that there is someone at board level to represent the supporters' point of view,' says Varney.

It's obviously a policy that works. Varney relates the tale that after the club's 13-match unbeaten run that sealed their Premiership place in 1998, the directors received a standing ovation at the company's Annual General Meeting. 'At most AGMs you'd be thinking, oh my God, what are they going to ask!' he says. 'I think people realise that the people running the club are fans. Fans and business people.'

Varney assures me that he has managed to overcome any conflict between his supporter's heart and his business head. It would be easy to fall into the trap of letting the former rule the latter, with potentially disastrous consequences. Whilst the supporters can rest assured that the club is in the hands of people who genuinely care passionately about the club's fortunes and aren't involved purely for any personal financial gains, the Charlton administration has by its actions and decisions allayed any fears that their business acumen could be affected by their desire for success.

'I think that as a fan I always felt uncomfortable with the philosophy that buying a particular player will solve an awful lot of problems, which is the mentality that a great deal of football supporters have, whatever their club,' says Varney. 'If that's the case, why are Blackburn Rovers in one of the relegation places? Jack Walker's got £36 million plus at his disposal and he can't turn the situation around just like that. I think I'm realistic enough to know that it's not just about going out and buying players, and I also believe that when you're running a football club you're almost like a guardian. We have to make sure that this club is still here in 50 years' time; that's the key objective towards which I am working. I don't sit here thinking next year we must win promotion, or we must do this or that. We must have the long-term aim that this club will still be in business when my son wants to come and watch the team, and his son after that. That's the main responsibility of any football club's administration. We're just holding the baton at the moment, and at some stage we'll pass it on to somebody else, so when we do so we want the club to be healthy and vibrant. And if you spend money you haven't got, then that won't be the case.'

Charlton's foray into the Premiership hasn't altered that strategy. At the time of our conversation, the Addicks were in the bottom three but still more than capable of preserving their position in the top flight. It wasn't to be. But the experience will have taught the club valuable lessons, as well as aiding their long-term position by sensible use of the income accrued from their turn at the trough.

'When I first came to the club in 1997, the discussions we had at transfer-deadline time were about selling a player to balance the books. We all sat down and came up with what we thought was a long-term strategy to turn the club around. We implemented a business plan, drew up an effective budget and all the rest of it. We thought we could turn the situation around and make money available for players on transfer-deadline day instead of working out who we could sell. As long as we were in the top six at deadline time, we could have a real crack at finishing the season strongly. Then who could tell what might happen: if you're in the play-offs, it's basically a lottery. So although we surged into the play-offs with a fantastic late run and then topped it all off by winning at Wembley, it didn't catch us by surprise. We already had plans in place.

'In fact, the Supporters' Club can tell you an interesting story about that. In February of what turned out to be the promotion year, we sold Carl Leaburn to Wimbledon. As a result of this, when I went around all the various branch meetings I was getting savaged because we were selling a forward, which meant we wouldn't go up and we had no ambition, all this sort of thing. I couldn't at that time tell them what was actually going to happen, so I just defended the club's position, telling them that I was still confident that we'd reach the play-offs and that they shouldn't write us off yet. At the end of the season, when we'd beaten Sunderland and gone up, I was invited to what was described as an 'evening of wine and humble pie', which was basically the supporters saying okay, you got it completely right and we'll keep our mouths shut from now on. I thought that was nice, a very magnanimous gesture by our supporters. I think they'd appreciated that they can trust us, that in the long term we'll get the club to where they want it to be.'

Having reached the promised land, however, the real hard work began. No sooner had Sasa Ilic smothered Michael Gray's spot-kick than the world was already damning Charlton's prospects in the top flight. Varney knew it would be a struggle from day one.

'The gap between the First Division and the Premiership is absolutely massive, on and off the field. There are obviously going to be added difficulties for a club like ours, and you have to be realistic. You're coming into a league where, for example, Manchester United have a turnover of over £88 million, whilst you're turning over £5 million. Bridging a gap like that is impossible. You have to be realistic about what you can achieve. On the one hand you have to be as bullish as possible about doing whatever you can do to stay in the Premiership, but on the other hand you have to consider the worst case: if we do go down, can we make sure we're strong enough to come back up again? I think where a lot of clubs have gone wrong is that they've gambled the future income from television to stay up. They've maybe had a manager who's gone to them and said, "Just get me this one extra player and we'll stay up." So everything is gambled on that chance of staying up, they go down, suddenly the wage bill is a bill they can't afford, people know they've got financial problems and they can't get the fees for players. They end up in the kind of nightmare scenario that Crystal Palace have found themselves in.'

Much is made of the so-called 'golden parachute' which clubs receive if they fall out of the Premiership. Many supporters and some club administrators see it more as a quick fix, a cash bonus to be spent on as fast a return as possible. Having studied other clubs' downfalls, Varney is wise to the parachute's pitfalls.

'You have to use that money correctly. What it's designed as is an acknowledgement that when you go from the Nationwide to the Premiership, your costs increase dramatically. If you are then relegated, that money is designed to protect you against those costs. However, what it's been used as in a lot of cases is stake money to gamble on staying up, which more often than not backfires. So when a club turns to use it for the purpose it's designed for, it's not there. Hence you end up with huge problems. We won't fall into that trap if we go down.'

As well as the increased costs of the Premiership, a club can expect its income to rise as well. At the dawn of the Premiership season, Charlton's capacity was a fraction over 20,000. The club sold 17,000 season tickets, and could easily have sold many more. A total of 2,000 seats were reserved for visiting supporters, whilst the remaining 1,000 were balloted amongst members of what was called the Charlton Athletic Priority Scheme, which was designed to ensure that The Valley didn't become a totally closed shop. Whilst immensely satisfied with the season-ticket sales, Varney admits that the limited capacity can prove frustrating to the club's ambitions.

'It is amazingly frustrating, but also it stands as a statement of how far the club has come. Premiership football has opened up a whole new market for us. We are now arguably the biggest club south of the Thames; only Southampton could probably claim that title. When we played Manchester United, Arsenal and Chelsea down here this season, we could easily have sold 40,000 tickets for those matches.

'Look at it this way. We've got 17,000 season-ticket holders, none of whom can buy a ticket for a friend. When one of their mates says to them in the pub, oh, I'll come with you on Saturday, they can't, because they can't get hold of a ticket. If every season-ticket holder brought along just one friend to a big game – and some would bring three or four – that immediately doubles your crowd to 34,000. I look around The Valley and think that if it held 40,000 people we could fill it. Not for every game, obviously, but certainly for the big matches.

'This club has the potential to be massive, and to compete in the Premiership you have to finance the team. We've submitted a planning application to the council for a new double-decker stand behind the goal which will give us extra seats. But that's going to cost us £4 million. That's £4 million that won't be spent on the team. But if that stand is built, it guarantees us a great deal of extra income should we still be in the Premiership.

'So the real challenge here is to balance the rebuilding of the club as a whole on and off the field, and achieving the right balance. Now I'm the person responsible for that and I can't tell you if we're getting it absolutely right. But if you'd looked out across this ground in, say, early 1992, you'd have been looking at a load of weeds, two stands burnt out and another completely wrecked. Now, just six years later, we're sitting in a brand-new stand looking out at a modern, 20,000-seat stadium. If that's what we've achieved in six years, where will we be in another six? We want to achieve everything, be it winning the European Cup or whatever, but we recognise that we can't do it overnight. We're building for success here. And if we keep progressing the way we are, who knows what might be possible?

'But for all our planning and ambition, it's still difficult to strike the right balance, isn't it? You might build that new stand and then get relegated, so no one wants to sit in it. But we're building positively on and off the field. The team certainly hasn't been disgraced this season. No one's turned us over, except possibly Manchester United up at Old Trafford; most of our games against the top clubs have ended in draws or defeats by the odd goal. So the team have done us proud and the supporters realise what it is we're trying to do, which always helps.

'Even if we do go down, and even with my fan's hat on, I wouldn't see it as disastrous. We've learnt a number of valuable lessons both on and off the field from being in the Premiership so we'll be a lot stronger and well equipped to come back up again. We're now firmly established as one of the top 25 clubs in the country, which you couldn't say two years ago, so that's a measure of the progress we've made. Make no mistake, if we do go down, we'll be strong enough to come back up again.'

The club have made great progress on the commercial side too. One of the first buildings to go up at The Valley was the club shop, a sign that the club were fully committed to a return two years before they actually did so. As the club and the stadium developed, it soon became clear that the shop had already been outgrown. It was demolished and the Charlton Athletic Superstore built. Not only that, but the old regime also went, staff who would stop marginally short of openly sneering at you.

'When I came here we still had an old-fashioned club-shop mentality. Almost a non-league type of approach: a hut in the corner where you can buy your hat, scarf and badge. In the modern game we have to realise that we are part of the leisure industry and introduce a proper retail strategy,' says Varney.

'What we found after doing our research was that whilst the younger fans bought the replica shirts, the majority of the older crowd couldn't really find anything in the shop that appealed to them. They didn't necessarily want to make the bold statement 'Look at me, I'm a football fan', so we introduced a more subtle range of leisurewear. We had the SE7 logo, an Addicks Leisure range, jumpers with 'Athletic' written on them. We introduced these new ranges recently, and hopefully we'll be making around one and a quarter million out of the Superstore this year.'

Varney also sees beyond the purely club-based shops. 'It is very difficult to change old habits, but I think there is a real need to have retail outlets in the community. Not just a shop, though, but somewhere where you can buy your match ticket and your programme the day before the game. Now whether that is something that should be done on a club basis or a retail basis is an interesting point. Football is very insular. This season London has six clubs in the Premiership. I would argue that it makes sense for those clubs to get together and invest in a venture where there is a 'London Football Shop', where all the clubs share premises and costs. This is very unlikely, though, because football clubs do tend to be quite insular in their outlook.'

Charlton's ambitions apparently know no bounds, and this encompasses The Valley as well. The club's years of exile during the '80s and early '90s forged a strong bond between the supporters and the patch of ground in SE7. The fiercely conducted campaign to return to the ground is one of football's greatest success stories. It's already well documented, but the longer the club stayed away, the stronger the desire to return became. Yet, despite the trauma and emotions of the 'Back To The Valley' campaign, Varney hints that the club might not be averse to upping sticks and moving on.

'I think that maybe there is potential for the club to move to another site, but there is this strong emotional tie to The Valley because of what has happened here. It would be very difficult to develop a stadium away from this site, maybe to one ready-made for you to attract the people in,' says Varney.

Without putting it in so many words, Varney was hinting at a rumour that had been circulating for a number of months: that Charlton Athletic were actively pursuing an interest in the Millennium Dome site. He seems almost relieved when I mention the name.

'Yes, well, there has to be a use for the Millennium Dome once it's done its job as the centrepiece of the millennium celebrations. It may be a natural sporting venue because it's geared up in that sort of way, taking into account transport infrastructures as well.

'It's on the agenda, put it that way. But with everything that's gone on here in the past it would be incredibly difficult to move. I mean, when it was announced that we were coming back here, we had thousands of people down here one Sunday pulling up the weeds and helping to tidy the place up. This ground is central to most people's memories of the club, and you can't take that away, can you? I mean, do people have the same affinity for a club if it moves somewhere else? Take Derby County, for example. When they moved from the Baseball Ground to Pride Park, I bet there were thousands of supporters who really missed the old ground, who still think, "I really miss the Baseball Ground, it's what it was all about."

'At The Valley we had all the campaigns, the political party standing in the local elections, we've watched it being slowly rebuilt almost like a giant Meccano set. So for us to suddenly turn round and say we're knocking it all down after all that effort would be particularly hard.'

A few weeks later, Charlton Athletic officially registered their interest in the Millennium Dome site, along with around 50 other interested parties. The club were quick to point out that there was no obligation in their submission; they were purely keeping their options open. The club's *glasnost* policy has led to fierce discussions in the fanzines and the local press. Most correspondents cannot believe that the club would even consider leaving their spiritual home, the home to where the supporters campaigned so hard for a return. It may be a measure of the club's ambition and business acumen, but that is scant consolation to those who saw the club's return to SE7 in 1992 as the fulfilment of the club's destiny. The importance of a sense of place, a belonging, an irrefutable presence at the heart of the community. Should the club up sticks and move to the Dome just to suit the few thousand glory-hunters who want to see David Beckham once a season?

Perhaps relegation from the Premiership has put the idea on the back burner for the time being. The register of interest does not commit the club to anything, but it would be a sad summary of the modern game if, after proving that football goes beyond money to a place in the community by returning to The Valley, the club then left the redeveloped ground for a site that was developed as a monument to ego and greed.

These are two characteristics that the Charlton Athletic board certainly don't possess. Indeed, they are a rare entity: an administration more interested in the club's health and future than personal profit. But a move to the Dome site to suit the occasional fans who want to see the big games at the expense of the regular fans who endured the wilderness years at Selhurst and Upton Parks would be a sad reflection of the priorities of modern football.

Supposed to Be at Home

Wimbledon v. Manchester City, FA Cup Third Round

One advantage of living in London is having so many football teams within easy reach. Boarding any London-bound train from south-east London on a Saturday lunchtime can sometimes seem like entering an electrical-goods trade convention. The logos of several computer and video manufacturers jostle for attention from the midriffs of every second traveller, whilst timid middle-aged couples warily await the inevitable outbreak of hostilities between those convinced of the superiority of JVC video recorders over Mesh computers.

In truth, the journeys pass in silence, fans occasionally flicking a glance at the allegiance of the person sitting opposite before returning their attention to the predictions of the experts in the tabloids, the empty cola can rolling around their feet or the person daft enough to think that the carriage toilet cubicle might conceivably be in working order.

Most of the capital's Premiership teams are represented on each train into town. The proliferation of Arsenal shirts perhaps still betrays the club's roots in the area before they left for the wilds of Islington in 1913, but probably has more to do with the fact that they did the double the season before. Spurs, Chelsea, Charlton and West Ham are represented, as well as a surprising number of Queens Park Rangers fans heading west. Crystal Palace, Millwall and even the odd Leyton Orient shirt can all be glimpsed heading for the tube station as the train reaches Charing Cross. But one shirt that you never see is that of one of London's leading sides, Wimbledon.

The Dons' swift rise from the Southern League to the Premiership has meant that their support hasn't had the time to catch up with their success. Crowds of 6,000 used to watch them play teams like Bedford Town and Guildford City in the mid-'70s; a few years later Liverpool were coming a-calling in front of the same fans.

133

The rise of Wimbledon was surely the most astounding football story of the '80s. From Southern League to the old First Division in just nine years – it's no wonder that their fans couldn't keep up! Imagine if Crawley Town hurtled up to the Premiership by 2009, carrying off the FA Cup two years later, and you'd come close to appreciating what Wimbledon have achieved. Granted, Plough Lane couldn't hold many people at the best of times, but tradition plays a major part in a club's contemporary level of support.

The move to Selhurst Park didn't exactly help, although the practicalities of public transport from Merton are not as prohibitive as they were for Charlton when they shared Palace's stadium. But without a traditional core support to draw on beyond the levels they enjoyed in the lower divisions, Wimbledon have not picked up fans from elsewhere in the capital despite winning the FA Cup and despite a prolonged stay in the top flight of the English game. I don't know any Wimbledon supporters. I used to know one, but he'd been going since the '40s. I know a few people who support other teams and go and watch Wimbledon every now and again. But I don't know any actual Wimbledon supporters. So who are they?

Arriving at Selhurst Park, I find a stadium barely recognisable as the one where I often stood on a windswept Holmesdale Road terrace with a few other hardy souls in Charlton's previous sortie in the top flight. It was always a characterless, bleak place, even on the rare occasions during Charlton's tenancy when it was full. With two nondescript stands on either side, one large bank of terracing behind one goal and a smaller terrace backing on to Sainsbury's supermarket, it was a featureless, unlovely ground.

Today, Palace have built two new stands behind the goals: a swanky two-tier affair on the Holmesdale and a smaller one at the Sainsbury's end. And it's still a featureless, unlovely place. The new home stand has 'Palace' and 'Eagles' picked out in the seats; this is the stand Wimbledon use as their home enclosure. When the City fans, who make up half of the 11,000 crowd for this FA Cup third-round tie, taunt their timid counterparts with 'You're supposed to be at home!', the irony is probably not lost on the Dons' followers.

On entering the ground I realised that I was in the City section. As it turned out I had a 50-50 chance, as the travelling City faithful had been given two sides of the ground. The crowds milling around outside all seemed to have Mancunian accents, and no fewer than three City fanzines were on sale. At least two souvenir stands sold City merchandise. Not bad for a team on the fringes of the Second Division promotion race.

Much has been written about the level of support that follows Manchester City: 13,000 season-ticket holders despite relegation to Division Two, and 26,000 crowds to watch Colchester United and Darlington. City are a club of tradition, the archetype of the fallen giant. City's pedigree is long and successful, and their crowds reflect that. This is not necessarily to their advantage, however.

Many clubs regard their vocal home support as being 'worth a goal start'. Unusually, City's followers are frequently worth a goal advantage to the opposition. Such is the desire for success amongst the City fans, stoked further by the dominance of their Old Trafford rivals, that the fans are on the players' backs almost from the off. The remarkable turnover of managers at Maine Road can be attributed in part to the influence of the crowd, who call for the head of the incumbent before his backside has warmed the seat if five-goal wins aren't chalked up in every game.

Normally, sitting amongst the supporters of a Second Division club visiting a Premiership ground, you would expect to be overwhelmed by enthusiasm, by the sheer joy of just being there. Not so today. City's fans have come here expecting to see their team win. The frustration they experience as the game progresses is that of a group of supporters losing to the underdog, not the appreciation of a battling performance by a team out of its depth.

Having arrived early, I watched as at the other end the 'Palace' and 'Eagles' seats were gradually filled by people purporting to be Wimbledon fans. Wimbledon's programme weighs a ton. Not because it has more pages than most, it just uses heavy paper. Even their programme has to throw its weight around. Inside, having jemmied the pages open, I came across Joe Kinnear pondering upon the previous week's Premiership attendances. In the accompanying photograph Joe appears to have just caught sight on the horizon of the man he suspects of burgling his house.

'The crowd at Elland Road this week [against Wimbledon] was their biggest of the season. Some 39,816 went through the turn-styles (sic). Not only that, but it was actually bigger than the crowd at Stamford Bridge that night to watch Chelsea take on Manchester United. I wouldn't go so far as saying we have greater pulling power than Manchester United, but you can't argue with the facts.'

Now, whilst Posh Spice would no doubt concur with Joe's summary of the Dons' and Manchester United's respective pulling power, I'm afraid I've missed the point that Joe's trying to make here. For a start, Chelsea's capacity at the time was 32,000, so it's pretty unlikely that their crowd would match Leeds's 40,000. And if, as he's perhaps implying,

135

Wimbledon are such a big draw, how come barely 6,000 arses are on the Wimbledon seats this afternoon?

Another curious aspect of the programme is the fact that when the editor sends the players their profile forms, he actually reproduces them, handwriting and all. Today, Carl Cort's random mixture of upper- and lower-case letters revealed that he would spend his last tenner on KFC. Presumably he meant fried chicken rather than investing in Kingstonian Football Club. Interestingly, under the 'boyhood footballing hero' question he had written 'never really had one'. However, the 'never' had clearly been written heavily over the name 'Ian'. Which Ian was this? Surely not Wallace? Botham, maybe? Lavender from *Dad's Army*? What made him change his mind?

I was roused from these considerations by the arrival of the teams. As hard as they tried, City's following couldn't raise much of an atmosphere at Selhurst. The Wimbledon administration had clearly given this some thought and come up with the following stroke of genius: every time Wimbledon win a corner, they play a rousing fanfare over the tannoy. As if musical stings after every goal weren't bad enough! You could almost see the Dons fans cringing at the other end. The first fanfare was greeted with hilarity by the City fans; the response to every one that followed veered further and further towards outright derision, particularly as the avalanche of City goals they had obviously anticipated failed to materialise.

Despite stretching Wimbledon's makeshift centre-backs Kenny Cunningham and Ben Thatcher, the Mancunians just didn't have the necessary penetration, save for a Paul Dickov volley ruled out for offside. At the other end, defender Andy Morrison was outstanding, easily the best player on the pitch. The match was settled on the hour when Carl Cort buried a Michael Hughes pass into the bottom corner. Seconds later, he contrived to miss a far easier chance to keep City's hopes of retrieving the game alive.

A dull game was enlivened in the last few minutes when a mass brawl broke out in the City penalty area. This always confuses the supporters, because, faced with a mêlée of players running around shoving and pulling each other, you can't really see what's going on. You don't know whether to egg on your players to render their opponents unconscious or call for common sense to prevail. And, particularly when the action takes place at the other end, you can't really tell who's winning. So when Cort and Morrison had a bit of a set-to and the rest of the players rushed to join in, the City fans had to content themselves with just a strangled shout that went something like 'Hhaaarrghhhfaaarggghhfoookinnnell-llllllgwaaaannnnnfooookinfoookinhhhaaarrgghhh!!!!'. Eventually peace broke out and Cort and Morrison were both sent off. Jason Euell joined them shortly afterwards, leaving ten playing nine on Palace's terrible, strength-sapping playing surface. Predictably, the game went nowhere after that.

City's fans left in a huff that a team from two divisions above them had had the temerity to beat them. The following week they travelled to Blackpool for the sort of fixture that attracts old hacks who can wax lyrical about how this would have been a huge game in about 1955. And isn't it weird watching a Blackpool v. Manchester City match that doesn't contain such classic individual battles as Stanley Matthews against Roy Paul? Answer: no, it isn't.

The Super Dons, meanwhile, went on to a fourth-round tie with Tottenham Hotspur, whom they played twice a week for about six weeks in early 1999, or so it seemed.

While this tie had its moments, the elusive magic of the cup has still to surface. I fear that I'm not going to find it, either. As grounds become increasingly characterless and FA Cup ties become just another game, even a minor irritation to the players and supporters of Premiership clubs, the world's greatest cup competition is fading, in the same way the League Cup has fast become an irrelevance.

Ho hum.

Orient Rearing

The Glamorous World of the Third Division Apprentice

David Parsons looks like your average 17-year-old. With close-cropped hair and a wardrobe full of casual sportswear, he could be a sixth-form student, an office junior, a trainee accountant or anything. But David Parsons is a little different from most lads of his age.

When most of us were kids playing in the park, we dreamed of being spotted by a big club. Much of the football literature available to us children of the '70s concerned a youngster kicking a football against the wall of the local ground. All of a sudden, the manager would pop his head out of the window and say 'Hey, sonny, why not come down for a trial?' and a glittering career would be launched. It seemed that simple. But the only reaction I used to get from thudding the ball against any wall was usually along the lines of 'Oi, clear off, you little sod'.

So when we hurtled around the park, skidding through dog turds and turning our ankles in the rutted turf, anyone showing the slightest interest in our games would be identified as a possible scout from a big club. The old boy in the flat cap walking his dog, or the middle-aged bloke with the pipe sitting on the bench – we all kept half an eye out just in case he reached inside his overcoat for a notebook and began scribbling whilst glancing in our direction. As we gathered our coats and jumpers and headed home for tea, we itched to feel a tap on the shoulder and hear the words 'That's a useful left foot you've got there, lad. There's a trial on at Stamford Bridge tomorrow, can you make it? Bring your boots and turn up at two o'clock.' I grew up in a house with a bus stop right outside. So whenever a bus stopped, there I'd be in the front garden, playing neat one-twos off the wall to dummy the hydrangeas and curling shots between the two cricket stumps that acted as goalposts, a little more upmarket than jumpers, just in case a scout from a top club happened to be on the top deck on his way to Lewisham.

It never happened, though, and long after the park years, long, hot summer afternoons in classrooms, lecture halls and offices would lead to imagined careers that could have materialised if the elusive scout had happened to be passing just as I clumped that 20-yarder in off where the post would have been if it hadn't been represented by a kagoule.

David Parsons has done all that. Halfway through his YTS apprentice-ship with Leyton Orient, he stands on the threshold of a career in the game we hold so dear. Having already suffered a long-term injury, he is familiar with the ups and the downs of the game and has already progressed further than 99 per cent of those of us who first pulled on a pair of boots in anger in the junior-school changing-rooms and dreamed of doing similar in the changing-rooms at Wembley. Whilst the average joe will have played on grounds no more salubrious than the local rec and, perhaps, a minor non-league ground in a local cup final, David Parsons has already trodden the hallowed turf of stadia such as Molineux and Highbury. He's also walked out at Wembley. The lucky, lucky sod.

At the age of ten, he received the tap on the shoulder that most of us dreamed of. 'Fancy a trial with Arsenal, son?' said the scout. And before long Parsons was becoming the youngest trialist ever to turn up at Highbury with a pair of boots.

'It was the summer of 1991 I think,' he recalls, 'and I did quite well. Although I was playing Under-10 football when I went for the trial, the youngest Arsenal team is Under-12, so I was playing with kids a lot older than me. Joe Cole was there at the time. We ended up at the same college and everything.'

Parsons was signed on schoolboy forms and stayed at Arsenal throughout his junior years. His debut on the Highbury pitch itself holds mixed memories. Having finally been given the chance to grace the turf where greats such as Ian Wright, Liam Brady and, er, Gus Caesar plied their trade, Parsons came on as a substitute late in the first half, but within minutes he was lying on the ground in agony.

'It was a fair tackle,' he recalls. 'Highbury is a lovely pitch, but the ground was quite hard. I went in for a challenge and immediately knew something was wrong. At first they thought it was just a sprain or some-thing but sent me to the hospital as a precaution. The X-rays showed that the leg was actually broken.

'I was out for a year altogether. For the first eight weeks I was in plaster from hip to toe, and I was in plaster for four months altogether. After that it was a battle to build the muscles up again, but the club were very supportive.'

During his absence from the team, Liam Brady took over the youth coaching set-up. Although Parsons was still at the ground, hobbling on crutches, the new boss never saw him play. Eventually the decision was taken that he would be released.

'We've no complaints about the way Arsenal handled David,' says his father, Norman. 'They told him they were letting him go at the right time of year for him to fix himself up with another club. Some clubs leave the boys hanging on until it's too late, and they're left without a club because all the others have taken on their quota for that year.

'If you look at the Arsenal set-up, they're very, very selective. They've a large network of scouts but very few lads are actually taken on, and once you're there they keep you on for a good while. Many other clubs have lots of kids on their books, even though they're really only interested in one or two. Take Spurs. They've got three teams in each junior age group, which is a lot. There's very little chance of a boy breaking through with those numbers. Arsenal have only eight to ten lads in a particular year group. I have to say, Arsenal do a good job with the youngsters.'

Arsenal's reputation for nurturing their young players means that those boys who are released are immediate targets for other clubs. The Gunners circulate the details of the youngsters not retained, and very few have trouble finding another club. Many clubs actively wait for the lists before deciding how many players to take on themselves.

'I had enquiries from 12 clubs after Arsenal let me go,' says David. 'That's not to say that 12 actually wanted to take me on, but they registered their interest. Because I'd come from Arsenal, this network develops where clubs phone you up for a chat. I went over to Queens Park Rangers for a few weeks, but the travelling from where I live was a nightmare. Also, the lads at QPR had all been together for a while, which made it a little bit difficult to break through.'

It was the personal touch that took the young footballer to Brisbane Road.

'Chris Ramsey from Leyton Orient came and had a chat with David and invited him up to Brisbane Road,' says Norman. 'We were very impressed with his attitude, and I'm not surprised he went on to become the coach of the England Under-20 side.

'It was a bit of a gamble on their part. David was coming back from this long-term injury, and as a result of the lay-off he was a little bit overweight. After all, he hadn't played competitive football for a year. But Chris Ramsey said that they were prepared to be patient, that Orient had a long-term squad in mind and that they saw David as a potential part of that.

'That made us all feel very positive. We've got a lot of respect for Chris and for Paul Brush, who looks after the youths now. They encourage the boys to get into good habits from the start.'

'The YTS is for two years,' says David, 'but there's no guarantee that you'll be there for that long. If they think you're not going to make the grade then they'll release you. One lad was released after about five months because they thought he had the wrong attitude.'

Despite moving from one of the biggest and most successful clubs in the land to one at the opposite end of the scale, David sees the advantages of dropping down the divisions.

'The thing about being at a relatively small club is that you really feel involved,' he says. 'A lot of the youth-team lads play regularly for the reserves, because the first-team squad is only 16 or 17 players. That way you can learn from playing with older, more experienced players and you're playing against similar players. The games are in the Capital League, so you're up against non-league teams like Rushden and Diamonds as well as other Nationwide League teams. The young lads learn a lot from playing at that level. And also, I find that you have a lot more time on the ball in the reserves than you do in the youth team, and the Brisbane Road pitch is one of the best I've played on.

'There is a lot of chopping and changing, though. It can be difficult, like if you're playing alongside a trialist from overseas. He might not speak much English, which makes communication difficult at times.'

In the 1998–99 FA Youth Cup, Leyton Orient were drawn against Wolverhampton Wanderers, a club with a big youth squad. The O's held their Black Country counterparts to a 1–1 draw at Brisbane Road, and the replay, despite a 4–1 defeat, provided David with one of the most memorable nights of his career so far.

'I'd played at The Valley before,' he says, 'but it was a whole new experience to play at Molineux. You walk up the tunnel and you can just see this massive stand in front of you rising up into the night. It's amazing. The pitch looks big as well, because there is a lot of space between the pitch and the stands. But in the end the pitch wasn't all that good – it was heavy and covered in sand – and we lost 4–1.'

The other advantage of being at a small club is that the opportunities for first-team football are greater and more realistic.

'The manager Tommy Taylor came to see us the other day and said that next year there are five substitutes allowed for league matches. He said that some of us were doing really well, so if he had a couple of injuries to first-team players or whatever he wouldn't be worried about putting us on the bench. I've still got friends at Arsenal who've been there for four or five years and they're nowhere near being that close to the first team. That's the difference between being there and being at a club like Orient.

'Overall, I would say that I've got more chance of making a breakthrough with Orient than if I'd stayed at Arsenal. Orient haven't got the money to go out and buy someone as injury cover or whatever; they have to look at what they've got. Over the season they've told me I'm doing really well and that if I carry on the way I am, I should break through eventually.'

Despite the depleted resources, Orient made it to Wembley in the 1999 Third Division play-offs. I spoke to David just before the play-off weekend. 'It's great that the club have got there,' he says. 'There's a really positive feeling about it all; it filters right down through the club at every level. The club are taking all of us up there, which is great, especially for me in my first year at the club.

'The manager always tries to keep us involved with the first team. There's no "them and us" attitude. We mix quite a lot in training, and the older pros are always willing to give us advice. Martin Ling plays in midfield for the first team, the same position as me, and we often have a chat. He's a big influence at the club, particularly at the moment because he's played in a play-off final for Swindon at Wembley.

'Some of the older players put in extra training after the main session finishes, and I think that creates a good example for the rest of us. You look at them and think, well, he's quite old now and he's still at it. What can I achieve if I keep working hard?'

Life in the Third Division certainly isn't glamorous. Wages can often work out at around £300 per week, which isn't a lot for someone well into their career. As a YTS lad, David receives just £45 a week. 'You get travel expenses as well,' he says, 'but it's not a lot of money.' He's about to learn to drive, but enquiries about insurance have turned up a problem not usually associated with the 'glamorous' world of professional football.

'He's having trouble finding insurance,' says Norman, 'because as soon as he tells them he's a professional footballer the premiums go through the roof. They're high enough for young lads as it is, but they say things like "What if you're in the car with Alan Shearer or someone and you have a crash?" – as if that's ever going to happen!'

So the dream world of the professional footballer isn't as glamorous as it seems. David Parsons wouldn't swap it for anything, though. A shy, quietly spoken lad, he was recognised by a fan for the first time recently, which he found weird.

Orient lost at Wembley. Despite the fact they dominated most of the game, an early Scunthorpe goal condemned them to another season in the Third Division. David says he's never heard a dressing-room so deafeningly quiet as the O's at Wembley that day. So if he does break through next season, it will be in the Third Division. He has one more year to run on his YTS before he finds out whether Orient will offer him a full professional contract. He's quietly optimistic.

'They've told me just to keep on doing what I'm doing and I'll do all right. They've said the same to all of us, which shows how well the youth team's done. I'm happy at Leyton Orient, yes, I'd like to stay on there.'

David has had the opportunities many of us would have killed for. His quiet modesty conceals a powerful determination to succeed. He has the right attitude. Orient's faith and patience with a crocked youngster from a big club could just pay off.

Football as Art

Wimbledon v. Tottenham Hotspur, FA Cup Fourth Round

Having spent most of my football-watching years outside the top flight, I haven't seen much of what could really be described as the beautiful game. Of course, if quality of football were the only criterion for your choice of club, the Football League would have ceased to exist years ago. But whenever I've encountered supporters of Premiership clubs, even if they live opposite the ground and have been season-ticket holders since before they were in the womb, I've always had an irrational sneering disrespect for them as half-committed glory-hunters.

I was a little bit suspicious of *Fever Pitch*. How could Nick Hornby talk about anguish and pain when he has never seen his club relegated to the Third Division? So Arsenal have lost at Wembley a couple of times. How tragic. I saw Charlton lose at Wembley once, in 1987 to Blackburn Rovers in the Full Members' Cup final to a goal from Colin Hendry in the 88th minute. Only 15,000 Charlton fans had gathered there that day. There wasn't any wailing or gnashing of teeth behind the goal that after-noon, just a slow, cold, creeping numbness, the realisation that this is how it is meant to be for a club like Charlton. The Addicks' promotion following the 1998 play-off final was unreal. We weren't supposed to win things like that. Nick Hornby saw his team win the league. He saw them win the FA Cup. He's seen them win the double. He's seen them win a European trophy. I've seen Charlton win a play-off final on penalties and lose an irrelevant final to a team from the division below at Wembley. To me that's what football is about. The torpedoing of hope, expectation being picked off by the sniper fire of depressing reality.

So, at Selhurst Park for the FA Cup tie between Wimbledon and Tottenham Hotspur, I sat among the Spurs fans behind the goal feeling like I was the only true football fan in the entire stand. Spurs fans don't support a real football club like me, do they? They're suckered into giving larcenous financial contributions to a greedy corporation in return for seeing a bunch of overpaid pretty boys flounce around in a plastic stadium for an hour and a half. And there's so many of them. One thing about being a Charlton fan is that you share your memories with a select band of people. Great moments are exclusive to our memory, not endlessly diluted by repeated showings on television. I'd almost be embarrassed to be a Tottenham fan. Or an Arsenal fan. Or any of the big clubs, come to think of it.

But, midway through the first half of this FA Cup fourth-round fixture, it suddenly became clear to me why the White Hart Lane faithful part with such ridiculous sums to watch their team. Just one fleeting moment completely changed my perspective.

This was the second of five encounters between Wimbledon and Tottenham Hotspur in the space of about four weeks. Seven days earlier, the two sides had fought out a 0–0 draw made controversial by David Ginola throwing himself to the turf whenever anyone in the crowd so much as sneezed. I confess to having been seduced by the Continental cliché of play-acting when it came to the shampoo-endorsing maestro with a particular susceptibility to gravity. The previous season, as Spurs lurched from one disaster to the next and were all but relegated, Ginola was one of the few players to emerge with any credit. But one tumble in the penalty area and it was back to the stereotype.

Predictably, Ginola was roundly booed by a Wimbledon contingent which had swelled considerably since the last round. A total of 22,229 people had packed into Selhurst Park, more people than had attended the eight matches I'd seen in the competition thus far put together.

I was put in mind of the play-off semi-final between Charlton and Ipswich the previous season when Ipswich's Bobby Petta seemed similarly bamboozled by the effects of gravity every time he ventured into the Charlton penalty area at Portman Road. No penalties were given, much to his disgust. In the second leg at The Valley, barely five minutes were on the clock when Petta surged into the Charlton box, only to tumble to the floor as if picked off by a shotgun as soon as a defender went near him. Barely ten yards away, three Charlton fans in the seats had come prepared, holding up cards with the scores 5.9, 5.9, 5.9. Petta didn't dive again for the rest of the match.

The catcalls of the Wimbledon faithful were countered by the supportive chants of the Spurs fans, and it soon became clear that this match was to be about one man's performance. And, around 20 minutes into the game, he produced one of the most sublime moments of skill I have ever seen on a football pitch.

Receiving the ball on the left-hand side deep in his own half, the Frenchman went to move inside. Three Wimbledon players immediately moved to close him down. Suddenly, he was past them and moving off upfield, leaving three Wimbledon players wondering where the hell he had gone. To this day I don't know what he did: one minute he was in one place, the next he was in another. It was almost as if the earth had shifted slightly on its axis and David Ginola was the only one who knew about it. Never have I felt that my eyes have deceived me at a football match, not even when faced with some of Carl Leaburn's astonishing misses. It wasn't a simple shimmy or a conventional drop of the shoulder. It was almost as if he'd just popped into a different dimension for a fraction of a second, just enough to bamboozle those three Wimbledon players and leave them facing a stand rising to applaud a supreme piece of artistry. Perhaps the fact that I was in the front row of seats, and actually seeing the move – or, rather, not seeing it – the same way as the Wimbledon players did made it even more stunning. When I watched the highlights on *Match of the Day* that night it didn't look so spectacular seen from above, but at the time I was left rubbing my eyes in disbelief.

Ginola was involved in everything Tottenham did. Unfortunately, so was Ruel Fox. If the flowing-locked Frenchman had served up one of the most astonishing pieces of wizardry I'd ever seen in the flesh, Ruel Fox was turning in possibly the worst impersonation of a top-class footballer I'd witnessed for many years. And at a Wimbledon game that's quite an achievement. Everything he did came to nothing. Crosses would squirt from his boot and pepper the ranks behind the goal. Carefully weighted passes would find touch or a Wimbledon player. Every time he went to go past a player, his opponent would whip the ball away and leave the winger kicking air. He was having an absolute nightmare. Yet, outwardly, it didn't seem to bother him. Many players would at least acknowledge a terrible pass with an apologetic wave of the hand, or hold their head, or stare at the turf in an attempt to fathom how any trace of ability had suddenly deserted them.

Fox, on the other hand, didn't seem to react at all. Maybe this was creditable positive thinking, or maybe he just didn't realise he was having a nightmare. Maybe he's just a cocky sod. Either way, the Spurs fans were not impressed, breaking off from their songs implying that the Arsenal manager was in the habit of offering sweets to small children in order to secure from them certain unspeakable services to berate the hapless Fox. If he heard them, though, he didn't take any notice.

Throughout the first half, our view from slightly to the left of one goal was obscured by a cameraman from Sky TV sitting at the pitchside.

Given the camera's propensity to block the view itself, you would have thought Sky might have picked a particularly svelte figure to man it. Not so. Giant Haystacks' big brother was blocking out the sunlight for around 30 people behind the goal. Complaints to stewards brought no solution. Despite being regularly told to keep himself and his camera on the perimeter track, the world's largest cameraman repeatedly heaved his bulk and his equipment up on to the pitch, thus completely obscuring the goal. One steward's explanation for his inability to move this gargantuan obstruction was that Sky had 'paid a lot of money to be here'. I'd paid 22 big ones to be here; the cameraman was being paid to be there. That's football, '90s-style. 'Well, for fuck's sake don't let him go to the tuck shop at half-time,' said the gentleman to my right.

The second half saw Wimbledon take the lead, only for Ginola to equalise with a brilliant strike, side-stepping two defenders on the edge of the area to drive a low shot into Neil Sullivan's bottom corner. Of the goal, that is, not the corner of Neil Sullivan's bottom. Even David Ginola isn't that precise from 20 yards.

Brilliant though Ginola was, however, I couldn't help feeling that today wasn't really about the FA Cup. Although more people watched this game than all the cup games I'd been to this season, it was sterile stuff. The magic of the FA Cup wasn't to be seen. This was just another game to the Premiership clubs, and this one in particular was just one instalment of the Wimbledon v. Spurs five-game marathon. To Sky, who showed the game in its entirety later in the evening, it was just another game allowing them to make empty comments about the greatest competition in the world.

The FA Cup just isn't what it was. Maybe it's because I'm a grown-up now, but the FA Cup was the highlight of the season when I was a kid. The third round, and the third-round draw, were eagerly awaited all season, with an anticipation matched only by the thrill of seeing the new programme design at the first match of each campaign. All summer long I'd wonder about it, even dream about it, but once that was out of the way it was then the long wait for the FA Cup.

Maybe it's because the grounds are more sterile. Now that Premiership clubs dominate the competition, even if you can get a ticket you're stuck in a seat watching sterile packaged entertainment. Clapton against Tilbury suddenly seems a long time ago. It's the early rounds that make the FA Cup the great competition that it is. The competition is one of the last bastions of football democracy; the idea that Bemerton Heath Harlequins can theoretically meet Manchester United in the same competition is one of the things that makes football great.

By the fourth round, however, the competition has basically become a bit of light relief for the big boys. Whilst the scoreline Aston Villa 0 Fulham 2 raises a cheer at Selhurst Park, such giant slayings are becoming scarce. And can Fulham's achievement be regarded as a shock, given the millions they have to spend?

As the fans leave Selhurst Park after the match, the talk isn't of who Spurs would like to meet in the next round, it's just oh bugger, we've got to play Wimbledon again. The only consistent thing running through the cup for me this season is that bloody Cher record which has been aired at grounds from Harrow to South Norwood thus far.

If this is the magic of the FA Cup these days, you can keep it.

Public School and the Offside Rule

Taking Tea with David Elleray

Not so long ago, referees were a largely anonymous bunch; figures in black on whom to pour scorn. If your full-back marred an otherwise faultless performance by slicing a clearance into the East Stand, a consoling murmur would spread around the ground. If the referee, on the other hand, made one small error, suddenly he was Judas Iscariot, Hitler and the Boston Strangler all rolled into one.

It was the anonymity which helped. We knew and cared very little about referees. Most of the time we didn't even know their first name – the programme just listed their initial and their place of origin. Occasionally it would offer a smidgen of detail, such as how the referee was an accountant from Smethwick, married with two young children, who enjoyed squash, walking and reading. We weren't interested, however. The referee was there to be shouted at. Any additional information was of little use, even as material to extend the abuse. 'You squash-playing, hill-walking, well-read bastard', for example, was seldom heard.

The advent of the Premiership changed all that. The traditional black kit was jazzed up, then changed to green, purple and any other colour that fitted in with the latest football marketing fad. Suddenly, referees became human beings. G. Poll suddenly acquired the Christian name Graham. D. Gallagher of Banbury became Dermot of that parish, whilst D. Elleray (Harrow-on-the-Hill) became David Elleray, Harrow School housemaster.

David Elleray is probably Britain's best-known referee. Others, such as Mike Reed and Paul Alcock, may have cultivated a certain notoriety for themselves, but Elleray is one of the few officials known for the fact that he is a top-class referee rather than for grievous sins committed with whistle and card. Before Manchester United fans spill coffee in their laps and launch this book out of the nearest window, it should be pointed out that he's had his moments, but David Elleray has, as much as a referee can, earned a good reputation.

I confess to having been a little apprehensive of interviewing him. Anyone who has the bottle repeatedly to send off Roy Keane and to rise to be a housemaster at one of Britain's top public schools as well as enduring 90 minutes of abuse from 35,000 people every Saturday has to be a bit of a tough character, despite appearances. I'd half-expected an arrogant, brusque, almost contemptuous person. Like, I suspect, most people, I'd assumed that referees have to be a bit power-crazy, picked on at school maybe, and out to gain revenge on the good-looking (excepting Roy Keane there, of course), successful, sporty ones that made their early days miserable. Control freaks, driven by personal and sexual inadequacy to nail down their insecurities.

When, through the startling inefficiency of the Metropolitan Line, I was a couple of minutes late for the interview, I feared the worst. From my research I knew that David Elleray is a man who prides himself on organisation. Combining schoolmastership with international refereeing allows, by his own admission, little time to relax. Every minute seems to be accounted for. When I rang the bell at Druries House, set back from Harrow-on-the-Hill High Street, and received no reply, I thought I'd cocked everything up. Having failed to arrive exactly at the appointed time, I presumed Elleray had given my window in his busy schedule to some more pressing concern.

The sound of footsteps on gravel allayed my fears, however, as the familiar cranium of Britain's best-known referee bustled around the corner. Clad in a billowing black academic gown and carrying a sheaf of papers, David Elleray apologised profusely for being held up at a staff meeting, shook my hand and ushered me inside.

The walls of the lobby outside his study are filled with photographs of Elleray lecturing or carding footballers. His 'rogues' gallery', as he calls it, is where the Harrow pupils in his charge wait to be summoned for a ticking-off; it could almost have been designed to intimidate.

Elleray's study is magnificent. The spring sunshine filters through the vast leaded bay window, which offers a view of the boatered, tail-coated Harrovians going about their business in the street outside. The room is cool and peaceful, a world away from the cacophonous cauldrons where the referee plies his other trade. The walls are decorated with more memorabilia, photographs and certificates, whilst a pennant almost large enough to be considered a flag is draped over the back of a chair, a gift from Barcelona to commemorate Elleray's refereeing of the European Super Cup final in 1998. The photographs are a mixture of Elleray brandishing cards and those where he sits amidst tightly packed ranks of schoolboys or stands proudly alongside ruddy-cheeked sports teams flushed with victory.

He employs a schoolmasterly psychology. I don't know whether he is expecting a grilling from me (I am rather expecting one from him), but whilst he sits imperiously behind his vast oak desk in a high chair, I am given a chair so low that if I pulled it up to the edge of his desk, my nostrils would breathe a misty cloud on to its polished surface.

Elleray switches on a CD of harpsichord music and disappears to make a cup of tea. On his bookshelf, the *Independent Schools Yearbook* sits next to the *Guinness Record of World Soccer*. A few volumes along, the bright yellow spine of the *SAS Survival Guide* is clearly visible. When he returns I ask him if the last volume is connected with his refereeing career. He smiles and tells me that it's helped him get out of a few Premiership grounds unscathed over the years. I think he's joking.

David Elleray was born in Kent. He took up refereeing in 1968, progressing to the Football League list in 1986. In the meantime he had gained a good degree from Oxford University and secured his first teaching post in 1977, housemaster at Druries House, Harrow School. Not bad for a first job.

Elleray has been on the Premiership list since its inauguration and joined the FIFA referees' list in 1992. He has refereed the Charity Shield, the FA Cup final, the World Club Championship, South Africa v. Brazil and the UEFA Super Cup. Not a bad list, but one with a glaring omission.

'When I started refereeing at the age of 13 in 1968, I decided that I'd referee the World Cup final in 1998 or 2002,' he says. It's an ambition he will not now realise. His age dictates that he comes off the FIFA list before the next World Cup, whilst other circumstances necessitated his absence from France in 1998.

'The school have always been very good in letting me have time off, but I couldn't do my job here and be away for the five or six weeks the World Cup would have taken up. Also I had applied for the headmastership here, and the interviews were going on during the tournament. It had to be one or the other.'

Elleray leads an extraordinary dual life. His job and Harrow School are obviously very important to him. Equally, he enjoys refereeing and meeting challenges at the highest level. The summer of 1998 presented him with the two potential pinnacles of both careers. For someone who is, let's face it, not exactly publicity-shy, many would say that they were surprised that he put the school ahead of the world's biggest sporting event. But Elleray has a sense of perspective: the fleeting glory of five weeks in France (and no guarantee of refereeing beyond the group stages) or the possibility of securing the top job at the school where he has spent his entire teaching career? Especially a school which has indulged his refereeing career with great generosity thus far.

'I like to think that when I am here I get all the work done that covers the time I'm away, so that neither the school nor the boys suffer. This means that, particularly during term-time, I don't have much of a social life. Whereas other people here will take half a day off, go out to dinner or whatever, I don't do that in term-time – my time off is the refereeing time,' he says.

For someone who leads such a hectic lifestyle, Elleray looks remarkably well. For a man well into his forties who has juggled two entirely separate careers, there are no signs of stress or worry in his face. Relaxation seems almost anathema to him, but, as he sits in his sunlit study with lilting baroque music in the background, his air is more of a retired businessman enjoying his freedom than a schoolmaster, housemaster and international referee.

'I don't relax very easily. I tend to get bored,' he says. 'I walk a lot, I go and see my goddaughters and I travel a bit. But when I go on holiday, I'm bored after about two days. I think I'm probably a workaholic.'

His organisation is almost inhuman. Although his study is crowded with photographs, memorabilia, books, papers, invitations and a large collection of ornamental frogs, everything has its place. There is no clutter. If you didn't know better, you'd say it was the organisation of someone with too much time on their hands (I didn't check, but I bet his CDs are filed in alphabetical order too).

His day job isn't even a nine-to-five forget-it-all-at-the-end-of-the-day occupation. As well as teaching geography to A-level standard, Elleray's main job is housemaster in charge of the Druries boarding house.

'You're there as a surrogate parent,' he says. 'Obviously during the term the boys are here 24 hours a day, seven days a week. They get two weekends off each term and a week's half-term away, so I'm the one who has to deal with their problems all the time they're here. I'm the person who says well done if they score goals or whatever, so I'm everything to them really.'

Presumably having a housemaster who pops up on television and in the newspapers at least once a week also gives the Druries boys plenty to dine out upon. But does being such a high-profile figure have its drawbacks? Harrow School is one of the pillars of the Establishment, the breeding ground for prime ministers, politicians, poets and diplomats, so is it just a little incongruous that Elleray is so heavily involved with what many traditional Establishment folk might regard as the heart of low culture?

'I don't think my dual life has its drawbacks in that respect,' he says. 'In fact I think it helps in a lot of ways because in the boys' eyes I'm not just a schoolteacher, I have got another life. Most of them are interested in football as well, which helps. Take the recent Arsenal v. Manchester United FA Cup semi-final. School started on the Tuesday and the replay was on the Wednesday. I think they rather liked the fact that they were sitting around the television watching the replay and their housemaster was refereeing.

'So we do have lots of discussions about football. I think I'm able to set them an example and show them that you can do a lot of things and do them well provided that you work hard and you're dedicated. I can say to a sportsman here yes, you can be a top cricketer and get top grades in your A levels, it just means organisation of work. If I'm managing to achieve that in my life then at least I am some sort of role model in terms of operating at a high level in all sorts of things.'

I can't imagine Elleray giving the 'dog ate my homework' excuse much shrift. It would probably be met with the same dismissiveness that Dennis Wise would receive when protesting 'I was going for the ball, ref'.

Yet despite the apparent polar extremes of Elleray's double life, there are a number of qualities that overlap.

'Teaching, housemastering and refereeing are very similar in that basically I'm dealing with people, and therefore I've got to be good at judging people's character. In the same way that you need to spot in a class of students, or within the house, the potential leaders and potential troublemakers, you have to do likewise with a team. You have to recognise those players who are the leaders, and work with them. Also you need to spot the one or two players who might cause you trouble if you let them get away with too much.

'I think the other way it all overlaps is that there's a large amount of selling yourself involved, selling your decisions and getting people to accept what you're doing, including when you make mistakes, so that overall you build a relationship with the people you are dealing with, be it players in the Premiership or people here at Harrow. If I can build up a reputation whereby people accept me and the way I do things, then I end up with an easier time.'

Elleray is convinced that his brand of relationship-building on the field is paying off. I point to the fact that he is at the bottom of the referees' league table of bookings and sendings-off. He nods vigorously.

'It's certainly not that I've gone soft or anything,' he says. (Denis Irwin, controversially sent off by Elleray for two bookable offences against Liverpool a couple of weeks later, would no doubt agree.) 'I think it's that the players have become increasingly used to me and the way I referee and therefore life becomes easier for us all.

'I've actually always been a strict referee,' he continues, 'and I've always been a strict schoolmaster. But however strict you are, provided people think you're fair, they become used to it. I'd like to think that when players and managers see that I'm refereeing, they realise that they can't get away with much and so won't try.

'I think if you do a number of high-profile games reasonably well and players see that you're going abroad and doing big international games, they probably treat you with greater respect than if you are a new referee whom they don't know. Most of the players call me by my Christian name, so to them I'm not just any old ref, I'm a particular person. As such I've probably got a certain amount of rapport and respect with the players before we start.'

Elleray is warming to his theme. This turns out to be one of the shortest interviews I've ever done. Not because I run out of questions, or that Elleray is giving evasive, quick answers; it is mostly to do with the fact that he is concise. In contrast to the long, rambling interviews I usually conduct, this one will be over in barely 40 minutes. Elleray's busy life enables him to answer questions fully but with an impressive economy of language.

'For example,' he continues, 'I refereed the Merseyside derby which contained the Robbie Fowler incident [where Fowler responded to the taunts of Everton fans by pretending to snort cocaine from the goal line]. The Merseyside derby is always a difficult game, but on the following Monday I was the reserve referee for the Nottingham Forest v. Liverpool match. In the warm-up beforehand, more than one player came up to me and said they thought I'd done really well on the Saturday. That sort of thing helps, so if you referee that team again, there is still a residue of respect for you. You can easily lose that respect if you don't referee very well, but at least you're not starting from a neutral position, you're starting from a positive position.'

It is perhaps fitting that as the game of football reaches arguably its highest peak at the end of the century, one of the leading arbiters of its rules lives and works in the place most responsible for their codification. Indeed, Elleray's presence in the middle for one of the greatest FA Cup matches ever played was suitably appropriate as it was a former Druries boy, Charles W. Alcock, who first proposed that a challenge cup competition be instigated for members of the Football Association. Indeed, the knockout nature of the FA Cup drew inspiration from Harrow School's Cock House competition.

The rules of the game were first set in stone in order to bring together the various versions of football played in the public schools at the end of the nineteenth century. On leaving their schools for the universities, aspiring footballers found themselves frustrated that their colleagues from other schools abided by wholly different rules. Thus the first laws of the game were drawn up almost as a pooling of the 'best bits' from the public schools. Harrow contributed, amongst others, the toss for ends, the kick-off, offsides and the banning of tripping, holding and pushing.

Elleray umpires Harrow football matches at the school, which are played for a few weeks each academic year. It's a curious game, peculiar to the school, where the matches are played between the houses. One can see how it was such a major precursor of the game we know today: it's 11-a-side with a goal at each end. Harrow football introduced the offside rule and throw-ins. There is a strong emphasis on sportsmanship, with the laws of the game stating, 'Rules have to be kept for the sake of conscience, and the benefit of the doubt is habitually given to the opposition. If you inadvertently break a rule, stand away at once.'

'I don't think Harrow football could teach soccer anything,' says Elleray. 'The only thing it has that people talk about in connection with soccer is two umpires, but there are no assistants as there are in soccer. It used to be that the umpire was there to decide any dispute – the players basically refereed the games themselves. That still goes on a bit. If a player is offside, the opposition will shout, "You're off, you're off!" and the player stops, which you don't get in soccer. I think it's a throwback to the more gentlemanly days of Victorian sport.'

The rules of the game have been tinkered with endlessly since those days, leading to a constant cry for consistency.

'There's always been a great battle in sport, and in soccer in particular, between consistency and common sense in refereeing and umpiring,' observes Elleray. 'Consistency demands that if a player commits a bad tackle he will be shown the yellow card regardless of when it occurs and who is refereeing. Common sense says that each referee should referee the game as he wants, which in turn leads to inconsistency.

'Over the past four or five years the players have demanded more consistency from referees and I think you now have consistent refereeing, but I don't think that means you can't have personalities in the game. I'm a different character from Paul Durkin, who's a very different character from Peter Jones, and so on. I think there is still the opportunity within the laws to use your own flexibility. Whilst certain offences are a definite yellow card, others are still up to our opinion. Not everyone would have refereed the Manchester United v. Arsenal semi-final the way I did; some referees would have given a lot more yellow cards early on to gain control. I tried to use my personality and my man-management skills so that I didn't, after ten or fifteen minutes, have six or seven yellow cards which would inevitably have meant two or three players being sent off.'

The early stages of a match are of particular importance. Just as a defender likes to get a crunching tackle in early to let the opposition forward know that he's there, so referees like to stamp their authority early on. Whilst some like to do this by throwing yellow cards around like confetti, Elleray prefers other methods.

'I think with very high-profile matches, the first ten or fifteen minutes are very difficult for the referee. You've got to hit the right balance whereby you deal with the bad things but don't kill the game. Equally, you have to get a grip on the match so it doesn't get out of control. That's very difficult; you have to be prepared to use your own self-confidence. On the "iffy" challenges that might or might not be a yellow card, perhaps you can talk your way through them. You want to leave some aggression and excitement in the game. You don't want to kill it completely and set a standard where because every tackle of that nature has had a yellow card in the first ten minutes, every tackle after that time does as well, so you end up with two reds and ten yellows in what has been a clean game. You just have to let the early storm blow itself out.'

Alongside the call for consistency has been the frequent call for professional referees. It's a concept often seen as the panacea for the game, a neat, catch-all phrase trotted out by managers when their professional charges have been allegedly robbed by a bank manager from the West Midlands. The prospect of professional referees was rejected by the Premiership chairmen in 1999, a decision welcomed by Elleray.

The first thing he does when I mention the subject is to correct my terminology. 'You mean full-time referees?' he asks sternly.

'Erm, yes,' I reply, suddenly transported back to the headmaster's study of my schooldays. I look at the ground and go red.

'We get very stroppy over this, because I would regard myself now as a professional referee in my approach and attitude. I'm not a strong supporter of full-time referees for a variety of reasons. Firstly I think there's a danger at the moment that people seem to think that if you have full-time referees you will have perfect decision-making. I think many people would like referees to be robots in the sense of never making any mistakes. But we are human beings, the same as the players, and they make mistakes. They don't get every pass right, they don't get every tackle right. Shearer doesn't score with every shot, Schmeichel doesn't save every shot.

'So the danger with full-time referees is that people would think that because you are suddenly paying referees £50–60,000 a year, that would somehow be the end of controversy, the end of mistakes, the end of disputes. But there are still decisions which are so 50-50 you could put a dozen people in a room, show them the video and you wouldn't get all 12 agreeing whether it was or wasn't a penalty or whatever. So in the end someone has to make a decision.

'I think that full-time referees would be under huge pressure. People would soon be saying well, we had this kind of rubbish at £400 a match, now we're paying them the equivalent of £3,000 a match. A full-time referee would worry that if he wasn't refereeing particularly well, not only would he lose his place on the list, which is always a worry, but he could actually lose his job, which could obviously affect his morale, and in turn his refereeing performances would suffer.'

Afraid to run the risk of receiving a sharp rap on the knuckles for interrupting, I let Elleray continue. I'm starting to feel like I ought to put my hand up before each question . . .

'I also think that refereeing is very lonely,' he continues. 'Unlike the players, you're not part of a team. You have your assistants, but they vary from match to match. You're basically on your own.

'I think the other great danger was that there was going to be only a small number of full-time referees and a larger number of part-time ones. You are therefore in danger of having a two-tier system.

'And basically I and a number of other senior referees were not interested in going full-time because of our careers. You would then have a situation where the full-time referees were not necessarily the best referees; you might lose some of the top referees from the game. If, say, ten years ago my only chance of becoming a Premiership, or First Division as it was then, referee was by going full-time, I probably would have given up refereeing. Now some might say that might have saved the game a lot of trouble, others might say that would have been a shame, but I think there are other people who wouldn't get to the top if the only way was by going full-time. You'd immediately reduce the pool you select referees from.

'Like everything in football, full-time referees is one of those nice one-line solutions to complex problems. In the end, referees are human beings who make several hundred decisions in every game, not always from the best viewing position, and they have to make those decisions in a split second.'

The increased media scrutiny of the game means that for a referee at the top level like David Elleray, every decision comes under the spotlight, examined from every angle and studied with the aid of Andy Gray and his computer pens. Just as great goals tend to stick in the memory less these days because, with a camera at every ground, you see so many, so it is with controversial refereeing decisions. Has Elleray noticed an increase in the pressure put on referees in recent seasons?

'Not during games, but I think certainly after games because everybody has an opinion. Because they've seen and studied every incident at length they inevitably want to talk about it. We make mistakes, inevitably we make mistakes, and now our mistakes are being exposed more than they ever were. This naturally puts pressure on referees.'

A fortnight or so later, when Elleray took charge of the vital Liverpool v. Manchester United Premiership clash, he denied United a penalty after Jesper Blomqvist was apparently fouled, then sent off Dennis Irwin late in the game which meant that the United full-back missed the FA Cup final. The scorn heaped upon Elleray was in direct contrast to the praise bestowed upon him for his handling of the FA Cup semi-final replay. One broadsheet newspaper published a cartoon showing the Manchester United megastore introducing a natty line in David Elleray punchbags. United's chairman Martin Edwards commented that if Arsenal went on to win the Premiership title, presumably they would be striking up a medal for Elleray. One newspaper called into question the referee's 'moral judgement' and warned that the 'cult of the official is upon us' and that 'decent, honest pros like Irwin' are suffering at the hands of this 'secret society'. Strong stuff, and the sort of thing that clearly frustrates Elleray.

'I think the great imbalance is that the criticism we get is out of all proportion to the praise we receive when we do well. The most you tend to expect is that if you have a good game you are not mentioned in the press reports. To actually get positive comments in the press is rare. Commentators seldom say "Now let's have a look at this again, wasn't it a brilliant decision?".

'Take those two semi-finals. In the first game a goal was disallowed – probably wrongly – because of a misjudgement by the assistant. The uproar went on for days. In the replay, Anelka's goal was disallowed correctly after an exceptional decision by the assistant. But he got around one per cent of the praise compared to the criticism the other guy received – he was crucified for three days for that decision. The assistant on the Wednesday makes a brilliant decision and gets no praise at all.

That, I think, is unfortunate and increases the pressure. The impression given of referees is always negative, and that's why people think that the standard is so low.'

I think Elleray is correct up to a point. However, spectators aren't at the game to watch the referee and linesmen, they're there supporting one of the teams. That's who they're watching. Most games see the crowd applaud a good decision (and not always sarcastically) now and again, but you will never see anyone going to a match to watch a great display of refereeing or linesmanship. Whilst the media are often over-zealous in their criticism, and sometimes ill informed as to the laws of the game, and the vituperation aimed at Elleray after the Irwin controversy was unnerving in its spite, it ostensibly reflects public opinion.

With the proliferation of cameras placed around Premiership grounds today, the use of video replays is often trotted out as another solution to the game's ills. Such a system has been introduced with some success in cricket and American football but is still to be experimented with in soccer. Elleray is not a supporter.

'There are two levels of decisions in football. One is the decision of fact – did the ball cross the line or not? – where you could contemplate the use of replays. A lot of decisions, however, are matters of opinion: is that tackle worth a yellow or a red card? In the end one person has to decide, and the referee is normally the best person because he knows what has led up to a particular incident. Take the Le Saux/Fowler incident [when the Chelsea defender laid out Robbie Fowler off the ball in response to taunts from the Liverpool striker about his sexuality]. The referee would have known of the verbals going on between the two of them which explained why Le Saux did what he did. Just watching on television, one wouldn't have been aware of that. Now that's not to defend what Le Saux did, but it demonstrates how the referee would be the best person to deal with it because he knows what has led up to the incident.

'The other problem with video replays is the way football has developed in the past decade or so. These days it is almost non-stop action. Again, the Arsenal v. Manchester United replay – what a fantastic game, almost non-stop football. If we had forever been stopping to look at a video, say to see whether Anelka's goal should have been disallowed, or to double-check that it was right to give a penalty, or to see whether Keane's tackle deserved a sending-off, you're disrupting part of the real integrity and attraction of the game.

'The area I'd like to use it in would be goal-line technology, because they are big decisions. I refereed the Chesterfield v. Middlesbrough FA

Cup semi-final in 1997, for instance, where, through no fault of their own, the referee and assistant were in no position to make a judgement on a big decision.'

Given the amount of criticism heaped upon referees, it's surprising to discover that at the grass-roots level the refereeing profession is in a fairly healthy state. A few days before meeting Elleray, I had got talking to a referee in the crowd at a sparsely attended non-league ground in north London. It turned out that this referee had just passed his class-one exams, which enable him to take charge of matches in the South Midlands League and to run the line in the Ryman League. When I mentioned to him that I would be interviewing David Elleray, he was unstinting in his admiration. It turned out that on passing his exam, this referee had written to Elleray for advice and received a courteous reply. He was obviously delighted by this, and hoped to enter into a regular correspondence.

'I'm surprised at the mailbag I get, certainly since my book [a diary of the 1997–98 season],' says Elleray. 'I've had huge numbers of letters from young referees who want advice. I have a group with whom I correspond regularly, and I certainly attempt to answer all correspondence.

'When I started refereeing there were referees I used to admire and it was always a thrill to talk to them. So if I can help somebody by writing to them and replying to their letters telling me about their games, hopefully that helps to keep them motivated so that if they have a rough game and consider giving it all up, they don't give up. To me that's giving something back. If you can help people out, it's fantastic.'

David Elleray obviously loves football. Whereas some of us who love the game choose to write about it, others prefer to spectate, many more to participate at whatever level. Elleray has chosen the whistle as his way of involving himself with the game he loves. We talk a few days after the epic Arsenal v. Manchester United semi-final replay settled by Ryan Giggs's wonder goal. It was a fantastic game of football settled by a sublime few seconds of skill, a goal unlikely to be bettered anywhere in the world. And David Elleray was in the middle of it all.

'I've been lucky over the years to have been refereeing matches that contained some great goals. I was the referee when David Beckham scored from inside his own half at Wimbledon. I was refereeing when Tony Yeboah scored the goal of the season for Leeds United against Liverpool. I've refereed one or two cracking goals from Ronaldo. I think the special thing about Giggs's goal was the context of it, that it came at the end of almost four hours of pulsating football over the two games. Manchester United were down to ten men and they'd saved a penalty in injury time, so to pull out a goal like that made it extra special. I was thrilled that it was such a fantastic goal and from the referee's point of view it was a clean goal with no dispute about it. The game was going to be decided on quality, not controversy.

'That semi-final was without doubt one of the best games I have refereed. When games go well I think the referee has played his part. We had three big decisions in the game: the disallowed Anelka goal, the penalty and the sending-off, all of which were proved to be totally correct. They were very big pressure decisions – to give a penalty in the 92nd minute which could decide the game is a huge decision to give. To feel that one had conducted the game in such a way that the players just got on and played football was a great source of satisfaction.'

Elleray rated 1998–99 as his most enjoyable season, but this was before the Manchester United v. Liverpool controversy. His season ended ignominiously, as he pulled out of the Arsenal v. Aston Villa match on the last day with a back injury, leading to inevitable claims that the referee had 'bottled it' in the wake of the hoo-ha. He hasn't long left as a referee and I can tell that he'll miss the day-to-day involvement.

'I think football has been very good to me,' he says. 'I've been involved in some huge games. I come off the international list at the end of 1999 so I won't referee another European final. I had to miss a course for the referees in the running for the finals this year because it clashed with something at school, so I lost my last chance to do the European Cup final. But I'd like to carry on refereeing at a decent level.

'I'll probably become a Premiership match observer when I finally finish. I'll certainly miss the adrenalin rush when you get in the tunnel and lead the players out. I won't, however, miss the training to keep fit, or driving home at three o'clock in the morning, or the hate mail and abusive phone calls.'

When David Elleray does blow his whistle for the last time, the world of football will certainly be a less interesting place.

The Cup Runneth Over

Arsenal v. Sheffield United, FA Cup Fifth Round;

Barnsley v. Tottenham Hotspur, FA Cup Sixth Round

I missed my first FA Cup game of the season. And with characteristic luck, I missed out on attending the one game I'd picked which had any bearing on the national consciousness at all. Struck down with a bout of flu so bad I was convinced that I'd contracted a tropical disease, I was confined to bed when I should have been at Arsenal v. Sheffield United. Well, I won't miss much, I thought. The Arse should see off the Blades without too much fuss. See them off they did, of course, but with a fuss that was fussier than any fuss that had ever been fussed before.

As I emerged from beneath a pile of tissues to listen to the reports on Radio Five, I heard of the bizarre events unfolding at Highbury. The story is well known, of course. Sheffield United put the ball out of play to allow one of their players to receive treatment for an injury. Ray Parlour threw the ball towards the corner flag, ostensibly to give possession back to United. Nwankwo Kanu ran on to the throw and centred to Marc Overmars, who belted in what turned out to be the winner. Sheffield United went ballistic, with Steve Bruce appearing to call his players off the pitch (his later explanation that he was summoning them to discuss the situation doesn't really stand up).

Kanu shouldered much of the blame on the grounds that he was new to the British game. And, of course, he is African, and therefore a bit naïve, bless him. It appears that some racial stereotypes will never be fully exposed as myth. Kanu has played at the highest level in Europe for some years. He may have thought that because Sheffield United put the ball out to allow treatment to one of their own it negated any obligation on his part to concede possession. He may just have forgotten. Whatever the reason, the media's focus on Kanu's role in the incident obfuscated

165

the part played by the real villain of the piece, Marc Overmars. Watch the replay on television: as soon as Kanu gains possession, the Dutch striker accelerates into the box to be left with the simplest of tap-ins whilst the stunned Sheffield United defence stands watching. Overmars ghosts past two static defenders who have obviously stopped playing, both within his line of vision. As soon as Kanu moves towards the ball, Overmars is away on his toes. Overmars knew much better than Kanu what the overall picture was, yet still he put the ball in the net and turned away to celebrate.

Somehow Overmars escaped criticism, whilst poor old Kanu copped the lot. Now some might read a racial overtone into this: if the roles had been switched and Overmars had crossed for Kanu to score, would the Dutch player have received the attention Kanu did? Or would it have been the Nigerian that was vilified for putting the ball into the net?

The match having finished 2–1, Arsenal magnanimously offered their opponents a rematch. At Highbury. Sheffield United could have argued that the offer effectively negated the goal, and by implication acknowledged that the match would have finished 1–1. If that had been the case then a replay at Bramall Lane would have been necessary, but Arsenal were having none of that nonsense, thanks very much. Hence Arsène Wenger's confused answer to the question of why Arsenal, if they knew they'd been at fault with Overmars' goal, didn't allow Sheffield United a goal back to even things up again nicely. That, said the Arsenal boss, wouldn't have been in keeping with the spirit of the game. A bit like Marc Overmars, eh?

And would Arsenal have offered a rematch if their opponents had been, say, Manchester United? Or would all have been fair in love and war? After all, none of the game's laws were broken. But it wasn't Manchester United, it was Sheffield United, from the division below. A team that would have difficulty psyching itself up once again for a trip to north London. A team that would probably not perform as well again against the same opponents. Any rematch would have been weighted heavily in Arsenal's favour. Instead the Gunners earned themselves a forest of brownie points for appearing to uphold the sporting ethos on which the game was founded. And Marc Overmars escaped criticism. Sheffield United lost the rematch 2–1, even though they had done enough in the first game to earn a replay on their own ground. At least they received extra revenue from their share of the gate for the second game. They must have been overjoyed.

Arsenal went into the sixth round, then, as did their north London rivals Tottenham Hotspur. In the quarter-finals Spurs were drawn away to First Division Barnsley, who had knocked them out of the cup the previous season before going on to dispose of Manchester United in the next round. Since relegation from the Premiership the previous season, the Tykes hadn't exactly set the Nationwide League on fire. But they had put together a useful cup run, and with a capacity partisan crowd guaranteed at Oakwell, surely this was at last the chance to see a good, full-blooded, old-fashioned scrap of an FA Cup tie. And I could watch it live in London.

Tottenham have introduced a scheme taken up by some other clubs of beaming back live pictures of away games to the big screen at White Hart Lane. Whilst this gives Spurs fans the opportunity of watching away games without the hassle and expense of away travel, it also proves to be a tidy boost to the Tottenham coffers. Why have your stadium standing empty just because the team is playing at the other end of the country? Why not show the match and charge for the privilege? At a tenner a throw, a couple of thousand fans nets you twenty grand, plus burgers and what people spend in the club shop. All income you wouldn't have had if everyone was at home with Teletext and *Sport on Five*.

This all makes good business sense: football stadia are grossly underused. But the Spurs project has thrown up some wider implications for the future of the game. Since commencing the live transmissions, Spurs have declined to take up their full allocation of tickets for some away matches, leading cynics to ponder whether the club are aiming to dissuade fans from travelling away in order that they watch the matches at White Hart Lane. Laudable service or cynical ploy to fleece fans of even more hard-earned cash? You decide. It looks as though David Evans's dream of stadia unblighted by the presence of away supporters may someday be fulfilled if this trend continues.

It's a bummer when you turn up at a ground to find that the match has been called off. Especially a ground where no match is scheduled to take place anyway. A blizzard had unburdened itself over Oakwell, and the match had been postponed. Pitch looks perfectly playable, I said to myself at White Hart Lane.

Instead, my afternoon was spent watching the last hour of Queens Park Rangers' First Division fixture with Wolverhampton Wanderers, as poor an excuse for a football match as you'll ever see. It was dreadful stuff, not helped by the fact that even though I'd missed the first half-hour (lucky me, as it turned out) I was still expected to fork out twenty quid for the privilege.

It was second time lucky the following week, however, as south Yorkshire managed to avoid any further unseasonal conditions, plagues of locusts and poxes on their firstborn, but I was still destined to miss the kick-off. Despite the fact that only around 5,000 people were at the ground, the queues were such that many of us missed the first ten minutes despite arriving in plenty of time. Having queued up for a good while to be relieved of a tenner (to watch a match on a big telly, remember), we were ushered through the turnstiles, up endless flights of stairs, along a concourse at the top of the stand, down another never-ending staircase, only to end up back in the street. This was pure marketing genius. Charge people a tenner for walking through the stand! Having successfully negotiated re-entry, we took our seats behind the goal in the South Stand to watch the big screen at the other end.

This was one of the strangest football-watching experiences I have ever had. I was sitting in a football ground, my knees up around my chin due to the proximity of the seat in front, and I was cold. Despite this, I was watching a match on the television. Not only that, but booming over the tannoy was the excitable larynx of Jonathan Pearce, whose commentary for Capital Gold was relayed across the airwaves to White Hart Lane. So I was watching a match live, watching it on television and listening to it on the radio all at the same time. Sensory overload.

The Spurs fans tried gamely to recreate the big-match atmosphere but, faced with 30,000 empty seats, it must have been a strangely soul-destroying experience. 'Come on you Spurs!' they sang at every corner. 'Ginola!' they chanted every time the Frenchman's phizog filled the screen. Which was quite often, because once again he dominated the proceedings. The game was sealed by a goal of characteristic brilliance: receiving the ball out on the touchline, the grey-flecked maestro danced all the way through the Barnsley defence to slot the ball past the goal-keeper for the only goal of the game. It was a goal good enough to bring people to their feet 200 miles away. Every replay was greeted as if it was another goal. Every close-up of Ginola's rain-soaked figure brought a standing ovation. A couple of hundred miles away from this unbridled adulation, thousands of Yorkshiremen were calling him a wanker.

Jonathan Pearce's commentary produced a strange phenomenon. After a Spurs move resulted in a corner, the world's most excitable man said, 'And that will have brought them to their feet back at White Hart Lane!' Unfortunately, the move hadn't brought everyone to their feet: 5,000 bums were still squarely on 5,000 seats. In response to Pearce's comments, however, everyone looked at each other and stood up in unison. If Jonathan Pearce had cottoned on to the strange power his words wielded back in north London, just think of the fun he could have had. 'Oh yes, that will have them cooking omelettes back at White Hart

Lane', perhaps, or 'Ooh, what a shot, that will have them all dancing butt-naked on their seats back at the Lane'. The possibilities were endless. Unfortunately, Jonathan Pearce was too interested in the football to try anything as daft as that. Bah. Might have livened the place up a bit. It certainly needed it.

White Hart Lane has been gradually turned into a sanitised arena devoid of any character. The roof joins up all the way around and all the seats are the same shade of blue. It also looks deceptively small. Okay, it's hard to judge when there's only 5,000 people present and they're all stuck at one end, but the Lane has definitely shed its character since the days of the Shelf and similar features. It also looks suspiciously like QPR now as well. There is nothing in the ground to tell you that this is the home of Tottenham Hotspur. The gold cockerel that stood on the fascia of the now-demolished stand is long gone. The views are all good, the concourses at the back of the stands are wide and clean, the food outlets are efficient and their board of fare highly palatable. This is the modern game and it's boring.

If this is the future of football stadia then I'll start to miss floodlight pylons obstructing your view, cardboard hamburgers and away ends where you can only see half the pitch. Surely it's possible to plan and construct a modern, safe stadium which retains the character of the club that plays there? White Hart Lane could be the local sports centre for all the character it possesses these days. I half-expected a couple of blokes to come out of the tunnel wearing badminton clothes and bewildered expressions, or an overweight woman in swimming costume, goggles and rubber hat to pad around the pitch looking for the footbath. We have seen the future and it's bland. Before long the Ninety-Two Club will only have to visit one ground because they'll all be the same. Seen one, seen the lot.

Nothing about White Hart Lane says Tottenham Hotspur. The ground meets all the criteria of the ideal modern stadium: excellent sight lines, safe access and egress, cover for all spectators. Okay, it's lacking a little in the leg-room department, even for a shortarse like me, but on the whole the Lane can be held up as a fine example of the modern football ground. The only thing is, it doesn't reflect anything of the club that plays there. It could have been constructed from a kit. It's an inevitable situation, I suppose. The character of a ground comes through its history. Stands on different sides were constructed at different times, by architects with imagination. The development of a ground reflected the status and achievements of the club that played there. I suppose if you raze the lot to the ground and start again, constructing a new ground to strict criteria within a short space of time, it's inevitable that the uniqueness of a stadium's features will be swept away with the rubble of the old construction. White Hart Lane is unrecognisable as the arena of the 1961 double-winning side. The push-and-run team of the '50s. The FA Cup-winning team of 1981. Even the ground where Paul Gascoigne played the best football of his career. White Hart Lane betrays nothing of what formed the nature of the fans' support and the character of the club that plays there.

On this night, though, the club that plays there was playing else-where. Towards the end of the match, something was nagging away at me. Something wasn't quite right. Finally I realised what it was. I hadn't moved my head for the entire match. Because we were watching the game on television, there was no reason to lean forward to see what was happening in the near goalmouth. There was no standing up and craning the neck at every corner. You could sit absolutely still and see everything, in close-up, with replays, and with the play being described for you over the tannoy as well. The complete football-as-leisure experience, in fact.

Spurs cruised to a comfortable victory in the cauldron of Oakwell. Back at the Lane, the supporters danced and sang in celebration of their place in the FA Cup semi-final. Half the semi-finalists would be from London; the prospect of a north London derby at Wembley was still very much alive.

So that was the big-screen experience. You could get used to it, I suppose, but then they said that about the poll tax.

Suitable Grounds for Change

The Rebirth of Tooting and Mitcham United

Tooting and Mitcham United's boardroom at Sandy Lane is as grand as you'll find at Ryman League Second Division level. The trophy cabinet is full, the honours board dominates the room and various long-dead dignitaries gaze at you from sepia-tinted photographs. The club's famous 2–2 draw with Nottingham Forest in the FA Cup third round of 1958–59 is commemorated in a photographic montage, whilst the all-conquering teams of that season line another wall. The youth team contains a jug-eared, fresh-faced goalkeeper called Alex Stepney. Ancient photographs show Tooting players wearing international caps, whilst a James Robertson-Justice lookalike, all curled moustache and neatly trimmed beard, has pride of place. This man, Jack Beard, was responsible for the amalgamation of the Tooting and Mitcham clubs in the 1930s. He now has a pub named after him, lucky chap.

The damp, musty smell of history lingers in the nostrils, although that could be the rain seeping in and soaking the carpet. You soon realise that you could have walked into this boardroom 20 years ago and found it in exactly the same condition. On the honours board, there is nothing listed after the early '70s ('Well, there's been a couple of things since that haven't been added,' manager Keith Boanas tells me, shuffling from foot to foot), and the trophies have a dull cloudiness rather than a sparkling shine. An atmosphere of neglect pervades the famous old club.

Sandy Lane is like an elderly comatose patient on a life-support machine. In theory capable of holding 17,000 people, today barely 150 click through the turnstiles on a Saturday afternoon. An imposing, if ramshackle, grandstand gazes across the pitch, whilst on three sides cracked, undulating, weed-strewn terracing banks steeply away from the pitch. Once a sumptuous amateur ground, Sandy Lane has the ambience of an old ocean-liner rusting away in a dry dock somewhere. The band of supporters who loyally follow the club home and away to giants such as Abingdon Town, Chalfont St Peter and Witham Town congregate at the evocatively named Bog End (as in 'We're all mad, we're insane, we're the Bog End, Sandy Lane'), and cynics might point out that the whole ground is a bit of a toilet.

For far too long Tooting and Mitcham United have lived off their name and reputation. Whilst they were once, albeit fleetingly, a major force in the amateur game, since the '60s the club have gradually declined to their lowly position today. Long-standing members of the Isthmian League, they are now in the Second Division, four divisions below the Football League. Despite the lack of success for around 30 years, the complacency of certain sections of the administration has led the club almost to oblivion. It has taken the fresh vision of someone without a historical tie to the club to blow away the cobwebs and set the club back on its feet. For Tooting and Mitcham United are about to leave the albatross of Sandy Lane for a new, purpose-built stadium a couple of miles away.

John Buffoni had been a Tooting fan for just four years when he became chairman in 1992. Bearded and greying, Buffoni has kind, sparkling eyes and an affable nature. A work colleague of the previous chairman, he was asked to become more involved and to help the club out of the mess into which it had sunk. As I sit with him and manager Keith Boanas in the boardroom, he unravels the tale of the saving of Tooting.

'I'm a figures man, really, and the more I looked at the situation, the more I realised that it was, well, I wouldn't go as far as saying corrupt, but it was just total and utter chaos,' he says. 'I thought, I'm wasting my time here. You had a system where you had trustees who owned the place who were also on the committee, and there was a little clique which meant that whenever you had a vote, the decision had basically already been taken. After a period of time I decided to turn it in, saying to my wife, "This is hooky." But I'm a political person, and my wife said to me, "You've always said you can't change anything from without, you have to change it from within. If you walk out now you're as bad as them."

'So I decided to put up against them and they all resigned, it's as simple as that. I said, "I'm going to go through the books [which were chaotic] and if I find any corruption I'm going straight to the police station. If I find mismanagement I'll draw the curtain down and make way for someone else because I haven't got time to muck about."'

Buffoni soon realised that the club had no future, financial or otherwise, as long as it stayed at the cavernous Sandy Lane ground. Immediately he put the wheels in motion to seek another more practical site.

'Basically, Tooting and Mitcham United Football Club owns the ground, and this is its only asset. Now at the time, in 1992, it was worth something in the region of £1.7 million. I picked out those people within the club on the committee who I thought had a bit of brains and formed what we called a relocation committee. One's an accountant, one's the managing director of a firm turning over £20 million, and we've got another one who, when all the brains are operating, is the one who picks out what you've all missed.

'We all decided that the only way to progress was to finish with the past and start again, because Tooting was just declining into oblivion. If the club had been sold, the money would have gone to the trustees. When I took over at that time the pitch had been left unattended for ten weeks and there was talk behind people's backs of amalgamating with Carshalton Athletic, so money had to be pumped in to save the club.'

Buffoni wasn't about to throw cash at the club willy-nilly, however. He'd realised how it would flutter away into the black hole of debt into which the club had allowed itself to fall.

'We set ourselves certain parameters. The deal we did with the developers was for £2 million, and we decided to spend no more than £3 million on the whole project, settle the club's debts, estimated at around half a million, and leave a quarter of a million in the bank so we'd go to the new ground financially secure. It's all very well moving to a new stadium, but if you're not financially secure for the next generation who takes over then it's a bit of a pointless exercise.'

Having set the limits, the club then set about looking for a new site. The option of moving in with a local school had some mileage but was eventually dropped due to the political machinations of the local council.

'I came up against the hard left of the council,' says Buffoni. 'That was right up my street, seeing as I'm a socialist, but these people were just stupid, you know, "over our dead body" and all this.

'Then we looked at Cannons leisure complex and for 18 months that was where we were led to believe we'd go with the council's support. But then they left us in the lurch. That floundered on one councillor saying, "What am I going to tell Mrs Smith who's walked her dog across there for the past 20 years?" My reply to that probably didn't help, actually.'

Finally, a third option came up, involving a football personality whose name alone provokes strong emotions.

'In the end,' says Buffoni, 'one of our supporters came up to me and said he was a friend of Ron Noades.' He pauses, smiles and continues. 'I say all right, go on then, you know, half-believing him. So this bloke says that Ron's looking to get some money out of Palace's old training ground at Bishopsford Road in Mitcham. Merton Borough Council will give nothing to Ron Noades, so he's willing to look at a lease option. So we went to see him.

'To be quite honest, we got on all right with him. I was still coming out afterwards counting my fingers after shaking hands with him, but to be fair to the man he's been up front with us, he talks to you straight and he's done what he said he would. You don't have to like him but that's how he is. I think he'd like to have his finger in the pie a bit more, but we think we're clever enough. Whether we are or not remains to be seen, but he's getting a quarter of a million out of us and that's it. I feel quite proud that Ron's only getting a quarter of a million instead of the £17.5 million he did the bloke at Palace for.

'Ron did say he wanted a premium. So I said, "Hang on, we've only got so much money." He just said, "Get it off the Lottery or get it off the developer. I've worked it out – that man's making a lot of money out there. If he wants to turn down another quarter of a million, I'll buy it." So we went to the developer and said there was another buyer interested and we needed this much more, and two days later he agreed. Ron was right. He knew the score.'

So Tooting and Mitcham United, having come out of a deal with Ron Noades apparently unscathed, took over the old Imperial Sports Ground, Mitcham, on 1 July 1999. The plans for the new ground are laid out in front of me on the boardroom table. It's an impressive scheme. The stadium will have a capacity of 3,500, including a 750-seat stand. The stand will encompass bar facilities, boardroom and a relatively luxurious home dressing-room. 'The away dressing-room will basically be a cupboard, of course,' smiles Buffoni. Wheelchair facilities will be provided, with a specially modified lift installed to raise wheelchair-bound fans to their vantage point. There will be cover at both ends and an all-weather multi-sports surface. It's all impressive stuff, and well researched.

'When we set about designing the stadium we travelled around every new ground, including Sittingbourne, who are in receivership, Dulwich Hamlet, who are also in trouble, and all these other teams, to try and learn from what they'd done. We've got the support of the local council, the opposition to the scheme is minimal and I know it will be a success,' he says, more with determination than with pride.

'You had the situation where a few people near the new ground didn't want us there, which is normal. They got up a petition for us not to go there, but the people around here got up a petition for us not to leave! We've always had a responsibility to the local residents. We could have just sold up to a supermarket, but this committee said no, when we leave this place we don't want to dump a load of hassle on the residents, so it was housing or nothing.

'But it's always a prickly subject, moving to a new area. One bloke down there said to me that there'll be 3,000 people tramping around pissing in his garden. I said we only get 150. I then said let's be fair about this, how old are you? Sixty-two, he says. Right, and have you lived in your house since it was built? No, he says, I bought it. So, I said, what do you reckon was here before your house, then, and he said a field. So I said well, if someone hadn't built your house on that field, you wouldn't be here moaning now, would you? Things change, that's natural.

'He then said what will happen if you draw Manchester United in the FA Cup?' At this point Boanas, a lifelong United fan, feigns heart failure and almost falls off his chair. 'I said well, I'd call a committee meeting which would last five minutes and we'd play at Old Trafford because of the money and the chance for the players to play there. I hope you're right, I hope it happens!'

Coupled with his desire to see Tooting back on its feet in more suitable surroundings, Buffoni is determined to see the complex used for activities that go beyond football.

'I've got Continental connections, so I've been abroad and looked at other clubs. These places are open seven days a week, not just for football but for social activities. I have every intention of opening the club seven days a week. If, say, adult-education classes want a space, somewhere to work, then they can use it. Take the boardroom we're sitting in now,' he says, gesturing around the room. 'This is used, apart from football, probably once, maybe twice a year. There are club members who've been here 50 years who've never even walked in here. The new ground is designed with the intention that every square foot can make the club money. If a local company wants to use the boardroom for a meeting or seminar or whatever, they can.'

The all-weather surface will be hired out as well, even to the exclusion of Boanas's team. But Buffoni has a public-relations masterplan in mind.

'I believe you only form an alliance with a football club through two things: where you live, and success. If Manchester United went down the pan tomorrow, all the kids would go and support Arsenal, wouldn't they? The man who'll be running the all-weather arena, he's looking at everyone who uses it paying a fee. But they'll also get a set of Tooting and

Mitcham home shirts and a set of away shirts as part of the deal. You won't make money out of the initial venture, but the value is that kids will be walking around Tooting and around Mitcham wearing club shirts.

'The potential is there: when Tooting are doing well, people come out of the woodwork, and we need to capitalise on that. But that's not my job, that's his job,' he says, pointing at Boanas, who puts his chin in his hands and raises his eyes. 'But he'll have the financial backing to achieve that. Our view is that we'll be one of the strongest clubs at this level, and we'll be financially secure. I might become a little bit harder than I am now,' says the man who came out of a meeting with Ron Noades with exactly what he wanted, 'but that's because all we've been doing up to now is surviving. Once we're thriving, it becomes business.'

Boanas, a former Stevenage Borough player and current Surrey County FA coach, is sure that the new ground will help attract better players to the club. 'It's unfortunate that it's not happening in time for next season. I think I've got enough ammunition to win us promotion next year. And that will help guarantee bringing better players in. Of course, the ground will be an attraction to players, and we'll have the extra financial clout to attract key players.'

Boanas's enthusiasm for the new ground is more outwardly displayed than Buffoni's. The man who put the wheels in motion to save the club is a little more stoical.

'Basically there is no hope of Tooting and Mitcham United surviving at Sandy Lane. But we're in a position where we can change that. We feel the aims are right for the club and there'll be a system in place for future generations. It's important that we get it right now. It's important that for the next generation Tooting is a stable, powerful club both on and off the field.

'We reckon we'll be moving somewhere around February. We'll go when we're ready, basically. We've survived for six years, so another couple of months won't make any difference. You only get one crack at this, so we're going to do it exactly right. Especially with regard to the pitch, on which we've spent £185,000. Keith probably won't like it because he wants to get in there. He'll have his view. I'll disregard it totally, of course, but he'll have his view . . .'

'It could be a problem moving mid-season,' says Boanas, having his view, 'but that's something we'll deal with at the time. It will all depend on how we're doing. We'll be training down there, and if, as I envisage, we're in the top three when we move, it should give the players an added lift. Whatever happens it should be a plus.'

The manager is obviously aiming high. He took over in October

1998, with the club near the bottom, and they eventually finished in the top ten with a creditable 66 points. Buffoni was satisfied with Boanas's first season in charge ('Although I don't want to give him a big head'). He also sees the move as a boost to the team.

'The players will be training there so they'll see it all going up. Sooner or later they'll be thinking, we'll be playing there, it's ours. Psychologically it'll be better than playing at what I'd call a bombsite like we do now.'

It appears that Buffoni has also succeeded in winning over the old guard. Many famous non-league clubs have been allowed to stagnate by short-sighted committees still stuck in a '50s timewarp where 5,000 people turn up for league games.

'I'm not an autocratic chairman,' he says, 'but I get things done my way. A lot of people don't like change, but I've managed to carry the membership with me. I've not done it isolated by myself: every single thing we've wanted to do, I've called the club members together and said this is what we're planning, do you agree or not? I even sacked the four trustees, but with the compliance of the entire membership, which you're required to do by law. We removed them because they weren't acting in the best interests of the club. At one stage they'd actually sold the ground without telling anybody. They had a mortgage through the brewery, it was called in and nobody told us. We found the money to take the mortgage over and then removed them.'

The realisation that football is now big business has taken a little longer to filter down through the semi-professional leagues. Many clubs are still run by committees of former players and enthusiasts. Many committee members are there purely for the kudos they perceive they earn. A number of the big old clubs (Kingstonian, Dulwich Hamlet and so on) have tried to move with the times, with varying degrees of success. Whilst Kingstonian are in the Conference and scooped the FA Trophy at Wembley in 1999, Dulwich are struggling on and off the pitch despite having had the foresight to sell their vast Champion Hill stadium to Sainsbury's and have them build a new stadium a stone's throw away as part of the deal.

Champion Hill was another famous old ground left to decay by blinkered administration as crowds plummeted from the early '60s. By the late '80s the ground was decrepit, even if it did have an imposing bearing. The club crest was set in marble at the main entrance, and the walls were covered with reminders of the great Dulwich teams of the past. Now they occupy a compact if characterless stadium, but are still struggling to make ends meet.

The weight of Tooting history doesn't hang too heavily around Buffoni. The latest plans for the new ground are displayed in the boardroom blu-tacked over an oil painting of Wembley Stadium in the '50s. Can't imagine who chose that location . . .

When the chairman pops out of the boardroom for a moment, I say to Boanas that it will be a shame in a way to see the old ground disappear. 'Oh yes, why's that then?' says Buffoni, coming back into the room. He's smiling as he says it, but the comment betrays his forward-looking philosophy, his desire to preserve football in Tooting for future generations.

The supporters have also been won over by the chairman's open, straightforward, no-nonsense style.

'Our supporters have got more money than the parent club at the moment. The first week I took over I called all the constituent parts of the club together, from the bar staff to the supporters. When I spoke to them, one of the supporters said to me if you run the club like we run our side, you'll be successful. I said is that right? I said do you pay rent? He said no. Gas and electricity? No. I said do you actually pay out anything? No, he said. Well, I said, I've got a four-year-old boy asleep at home, and when he wakes up in the morning, even he could make a profit with no fucking overheads, so don't give me a fucking lecture on money, right?

'When I first arrived, 20 people walked through the gate for nothing because they were on the supporters' club committee. I asked them what they were doing and they said they'd always done it. Not any more they don't.'

Treating long-standing supporters that way may sound harsh, but what Buffoni realised was that the supporters' club was part of the malaise dragging the club down. Although they were turning up to games, their contribution was almost nil. In fact, the club was even losing money at the gate through the number of freeloaders walking in for nothing. It was a situation he wasn't prepared to contemplate. Nor will he tolerate a less-than-professional attitude at Bishopsford Road.

'There are elements there who realise that things have to change', he says. 'But a lot of them are there for their own benefit, although they're allied to the club. I've said to them I want the standard of merchandise upgraded. The tea bars will be taken over by the franchise who'll do all the food in the ground. I said if you lot think you're going to take that hut full of botulism gear to the new ground, you've got another think coming. It's going to cost you. You'll pay all your overheads, because we're not a charity any more. So they've come to the conclusion that they don't want to run that side of it any more.

'I've said to them that the club will fund the upgraded merchandise like scarves and replica shirts and provide the supporters' club with an outlet so they don't need money. They can still run the 'Golden Goal' and make forty quid a match, and whatever they charge for membership, but every part of that operation will come into the club. That way I'll find out if they're real supporters or not, or if they're just in it for the money.

'That's not me being vindictive, it's just another example of how the club was set in its ways. Clubs at this level are generally run by old men who've been doing it for 45 years or whatever. Tooting is an example of what happens if you don't change with the times. Things change. We're semi-professional. We're no longer putting ten bob in the players' boots after every game, it's business. Players here today wouldn't move for five pound. Much as I don't like it, it's a fact of life we have to live with. The finance was all over the place when I came here. The debt is up to £500,000, and you can't service a debt like that. You have to get rid of it, don't you? And I'll make sure we do. We'll be debt-free, with money in the bank, a new stadium and a business plan that works.'

Tooting's sudden potential has caused a number of bees to hover around the potential honeypot going up at Bishopsford Road.

'There's been an awful lot of interest shown from, let's say, unusual quarters,' says Buffoni mysteriously. (Colombian drug barons? Saddam Hussein? Rupert Murdoch?) 'A lot of people have approached us. I said to one person who came here promising this, that and the other, well, give us the money now. He couldn't believe it. I said I need the money now, not when we've moved. When we've moved we'll have money. I need support and sponsorship now.

'Hopefully we will attract a major sponsor, and we'll be appointing a commercial manager. Obviously the gate money's a separate thing. We'll set that aside as, depending on the success of the team, any increase in gate money will go into the wage system. After we've got it, not before.'

Boanas raises his eyes again. I ask him whether he can envisage Conference football in the next decade.

'I wouldn't be in the job if I wasn't aiming high,' he says. 'Realistically, I don't think it's impossible to win continued promotion over the next three or four years. That has to be the target.'

Buffoni interjects. 'I think truthfully the members would be happy with Isthmian Premier Division football. To go into the Conference would require a lot of rethinking. It would be a big financial commitment. It shouldn't be beyond us, though. Mind you, Keith's got two years to get us into the Premier,' he winks with a sideways glance at the manager.

'Yeah,' says Boanas, 'and when we're top of that he's going to tell me to lose the last three games, isn't he?'

'I was upset when we were relegated to the Second Division,' continues the chairman, 'but in a way it probably wasn't such a bad thing because we've done a lot of restructuring. For example, you go away and a lot of clubs will just dump a plate of sandwiches on the boardroom table. Yet here it was like a banquet. I soon stopped that. Now if a club lays on a plate of sandwiches, that's what they'll get here. Take Billericay Town. They used to bring a coach when they played against us because they knew they were going to get fed. Like locusts they were. There were more people in here than out there, all eating our food. That's an example. We're not a pushover any more.

'That's not to say we're not a friendly club. We had a little team come here in the Surrey Senior Cup, Lingfield. Their officials arrived in a minibus and the players had to make their own way. They said it was the biggest day in their history, playing at Tooting and Mitcham, and I loved that. I think that sort of thing should be encouraged. Well, until we got on the pitch that is. I thought we could lose it – they were all over us. We won 2–0 and their people were still here at one o'clock in the morning, and they were having a great time. It got quite funny in here – everyone was friends and we're going to play them pre-season. Anyway, when we counted up the receipts it turned out that their share of the gate was 60 pence, because there was hardly anyone here. So I sent their chairman a letter saying we owe you 60 pence, that works out at half a lager, so if you want to come and claim it, let me know!'

He bends over backwards to be approachable. 'I said to my committee, you should be available for anybody to talk to, and if you can't answer any question, send them to me. I don't mean to say that I'm going to waste my time talking to an idiot, but if it's a genuine question about the future of the club, then come forward.

'All along we've held meetings with the supporters, Keith'll tell you we get tremendous noisy support home and away. People like playing against us because where they'd normally get 25 supporters, we'll turn up and it'll be 100.

'Anyway, the supporters have been great. There was one who'd sat down and worked out a list of ideas and suggestions and 75 per cent of them were really good. I mean, you've got these people they call groundhoppers, haven't you, and they'll all want to see the last game. We had loads at our last home game of the season because they thought that was it. There was an extra 200-odd. It wasn't the last game, but we never told them that. But this supporter says let's have last-day covers for Sandy

Lane and first-day covers for Bishopsford Road. Now that's a good idea, because there are nutters at this level who'll buy anything.

'He did go a bit far, mind. He said could we have a section of the corrugated fence at the Bog End placed in one of the perimeter walls to make us feel at home? I said oh, shut up! But we are good at PR like that. If someone wants to talk to me, of course I'll sit down and have a drink with them. A man came over from Australia who used to live in Tooting. His father coached one of the teams up here on the wall, so I brought him in, he's got the old camcorder going and there's tears in his eyes. So I made him some copies of the pictures and sent them out to him. Not too long ago there's no way that would have happened because this boardroom was like an inner sanctum or something. No one was allowed in.

'Now we've got a bloke who runs a website for us, and at the last count there'd been 18,000 people visiting it. If you go and lie on a beach in Spain, I guarantee that within five yards there'll be a Tooting supporter. It's incredible.'

'They wanted to change the name of the entrance road to Sandy Lane as well,' says Boanas. 'They're talking to the council and everything.'

'Yes, and all this sort of thing is constructive,' continues the chairman. 'They've taken time and trouble over doing it. But as I said to the committee, if you feel you're just going to move all this to over there and carry on the same way, your best bet is to pack up your bags and go, because this system has failed.'

John Buffoni has his head firmly screwed on. It would be wrong to give the impression that he didn't care about Tooting's history. He's hoping to bring Nottingham Forest down for the opening game at the new ground to recreate the 1959 FA Cup tie. It's rather that he recognises that the historical significance of Tooting and Mitcham is precisely what's holding the club back. As long as they play at Sandy Lane, that vast, crumbling white elephant, the less chance there is to exorcise the ghosts of the past and look to the future. Buffoni's vision is a lesson for football, particularly at the lower levels. Modern finance means that you cannot live beyond your means and on long-jettisoned reputations. He's not out for any personal glory – the ground will certainly not be named the John Buffoni Stadium – but he's obviously a great fan of the game who wants to ensure that it is preserved in the area. Particularly as, following Wimbledon's departure, Tooting and Mitcham United is the senior club in the London Borough of Merton.

'The way I look at it, at this level there are a lot of people who get involved because they like to have this little name tag: I'm this at

Dulwich, I'm that at Tooting. Well, I haven't got that ego trip. I wouldn't say that I'm a forceful chairman; I'm not interested in glad-handing people I don't like. I would love to wander down here on a Sunday morning and see a thousand kids playing football and the bar packed out and not one sod knowing who I am.'

Like a non-league troubleshooter, John Buffoni has shaken Tooting and Mitcham United out of complacency and launched what amounts to a new club. As the bulldozers rev their engines outside Sandy Lane and another London field disappears, a new vibrancy permeates through the club. Tooting and Mitcham United are alive and well.

Get Another Round In

Arsenal v. Manchester United, FA Cup Semi-Final Replay

Since Rupert Murdoch propped up his ailing satellite-television industry by securing rights to the Premiership in the early '90s, a new breed of football supporter has developed. A supporter to whom the modern game appears to be tailored, at the expense of those of us who go to matches. A supporter who doesn't have to go to the matches any more, which in the case of many Premiership clubs isn't possible anyway without a season ticket. Not committed enough to shell out the amounts equivalent to the national debt of a Central American country to secure such a ticket, yet still wishing to keep tabs on the progress of his or her team, this new breed of fan has found the perfect environment to enjoy the match in the company of others without running the gauntlet of public transport, appalling catering, overpriced programmes and ear-splitting tannoys.

The British pub is often mooted as one of those institutions that made Britain great. The foaming pint served by a comely, ruddy-cheeked wench ample of bosom in order to accommodate the heart of gold which beats therein was, to many, the backbone of the nation. Cheap stimuli for the horny-handed toiler of the soil and wage slave of industry could be found within the Red Lion, Rose and Crown or King's Arms. A few hours' escapism for a few shillings.

In the days of industry, football was a Saturday-afternoon experience which attracted working-class men in their thousands to the nation's grounds. The factory whistle would blow on a Saturday lunchtime and the masses would down tools, head to the local public house for a couple of pints and then congregate *en masse* at the local football stadium before returning to the pub for the evening. Sundays were for church and bathing.

Now that Britain's industrial prowess is rather less marked, the traditional Saturday-afternoon pursuit has devolved into a leisure experience available most nights of the week. Shorter working hours and a higher standard of living have meant increased profits for those involved in leisure as the workforce has more money to spend on it and more time to spend it in.

Today, the picture is rather different from that of just a few years ago. Football and pubs are at the heart of the leisure industry. The transformation of Britain from blue- to white-collar industry has caused this industry to explode. In the modern climate, a night in the pub is a costly experience. The British pub with its unique character has largely disappeared, replaced by cavernous drinking dens devoid of character and designed to relieve as many people as possible of as much cash as possible in the quickest time. A bit like football stadia, really. Perhaps the marriage of the pub and football was inevitable.

Many pubs now flourish purely due to the big canvas screen in the corner. Indeed, during the 1998 World Cup, the Wetherspoon chain, which had refused to show the World Cup in order to cater for those who weren't interested in the game, announced a dip in expected profits of £1 million over the period of the tournament. One pub in the Midlands has even constructed a replica bank of terracing complete with crush barrier to recreate that big-match atmosphere in front of the big screen as a small number of moneyed giants do battle for the benefit of a few thousand half-interested punters across the nation.

The days of people supporting their local teams because that was the only way to see a game of football are long gone. The modern football supporter is now seduced by success and glamour rather than the practicalities of local transport. Why support Gillingham, Chester City or Mansfield Town when you can attach your allegiance to Manchester United, whose matches are live on TV and who even have their own channel to keep you up to speed with events at Old Trafford?

For many people, watching matches in the pub on Sky beats the real thing in so many ways. Whilst you're still not guaranteed to see a thrilling contest, you can at least be sure that the best players in the land will be on show. No worries about the weather, about parking, about queuing for the toilets, about being assailed by rival fans. The pub fan can watch the match in comfort and warmth, with a constant supply of drinks and snacks at close hand.

The Arsenal v. Manchester United FA Cup semi-final replay of 1999 was probably the greatest match of the season. Ten years ago, it would have been the match of the century, but with the television saturation of the game our senses have been numbed by an overload of great matches and moments which have diluted our perception of the truly great occasions. But this match stood out from the rest because it had everything: players on the top of their game giving their all. It was a match played at frantic speed, packed with incident and settled at the death by one of the greatest goals ever scored. With a sense of duty and devotion second to none, I watched it in the pub.

The Coach and Horses in the London Borough of Bexley is as close as you'll come to a truly old-fashioned pub. Dating back to the 1760s, its décor is traditional (i.e. in need of renewal), its oak beams are decorated with hand-painted gold-leaf lettering and its landlord is a miserable bugger. It's not a particularly busy pub, but trade noticeably picks up when there's football on. Particularly when it's on Sky.

Tonight, a crowd of predominantly young men has gathered to watch the events unfolding at Villa Park. Most of them are drinking lager, a few are drinking lager tops. They are all backing Arsenal, even though there are no actual Arsenal fans amongst their number. They crowd around one of the two television sets in the pub. A few minutes before kick-off, a stubbly-chinned Irishman walks up to the bar and asks quietly whether the match is being shown. He takes his lager and lime and sits alone. It turns out that he is the only Manchester United fan in the building.

The events of the match are well documented. Dennis Bergkamp sees a late penalty saved by Peter Schmeichel to send the match into extra time, allowing Ryan Giggs to score one of the greatest goals ever seen to secure the red menace a place in the FA Cup final and keep their dreams of the treble alive. It appears that the FA Cup still has some of the old pizzazz after all. Not only is this undoubtedly one of the greatest cup ties of the season (although Bedlington Terriers may beg to differ on that one), it's also probably the match of the season in any competition. Although I suspect that Sky turn up the crowd volume to make the atmosphere sound better than it really is, the crowd were in fine voice also. The sedentary spectators in this genteel corner of south-east London manage to keep themselves in check, however. There's the odd frustrated shout of 'Come on, Arsenal' and the occasional loud exhale when a move breaks down or a chance goes begging. As Bergkamp's penalty is saved, one person shouts 'Fucking hell!' in despair. When Giggs scores his wonder goal, someone else shouts 'Fucking hell!' in amazement. No one leaps around when the goals go in.

At the other end of the pub, meanwhile, the lone United fan is turning himself inside out. When David Elleray points to the United penalty spot two minutes into injury time, he wraps his arms around his head in despair. When Schmeichel saves Bergkamp's effort, he raises both

185

fists in the air and lets out a little yelp. The Arsenal-backing cockneys glance over in his direction.

The yelp is emitted again when Giggs lashes the ball into the roof of the net for the extra-time decider. The final whistle goes and the Arsenal boys drain their pints, stand up and depart. The United fan switches to large vodkas and looks like he's been through the emotional spin-dryer.

And this is the future of football. I recall driving home from a match one night during the season listening to a radio phone-in about the proposed Murdoch takeover of Manchester United. I nearly swerved off the road when the presenter read out an e-mail from a Sky subscriber who said that it was people like him paying their Sky subscriptions that make the game what it is today. They are the modern fans, and anyone who didn't like it, well, their opinions don't count any more. It's Sky's money that has put the English game where it is today, and the Sky subscribers who fund the company with their little set-top boxes and four-packs of lager are now more important than those of us who actually go to the matches.

Whilst my immediate reaction was to telephone the radio station and challenge this correspondent to a fistfight, I soon realised that he was essentially correct. He'd put into as many words what everyone has slowly come to realise over recent years. The shifted kick-offs, the rearranged matches – it's all for the benefit of people sitting at home in their armchairs with the remote control dangling from their hands and the lager-drinking neutrals parked in the public houses of Britain. Football has become a televisual rather than a live phenomenon. Whilst this is a reflection of the way society has come to depend largely upon the crystal bucket in the corner of the room for social stimulation rather than a football-specific issue, it doesn't make it any less ominous for the future of the game.

Walk along any suburban street any midweek evening looking through the sitting-room windows as you pass. Whoops, mind that lamppost there. Before you are arrested for casing houses, you'll see families, couples and individuals with sullen expressions, glassily staring at the screen. This is leisure at the end of the twentieth century: watching television at home or in the pub. And by extension that means watching football in those locations as well.

Most people would say that this is hardly an earth-shattering revelation, and they'd be right, but it's this new breed of pub-fan that really drives home the dominance that television has over the game. They don't crave the live football experience, they just want to see the big names. The Premiership is what it's all about, the Nationwide League is irrelevant. Why peer at a programme when the Carling Opta statistics are flashing up on screen? Why drink weak, tasteless tea and chomp on a tasteless hot dog when you can reach out and purchase chilled beer and a plate of scampi without even leaving your seat?

It all makes sense as well. Football is a leisure experience, akin to going to the cinema or the theatre. It used to be something different, something you were passionate about. The FA Cup was about history, the thrill of the pre-match tension, counting down the days between the draw being made and the match itself.

Television has made the big clubs financially successful beyond belief, their teams have become stronger and the gulf between those teams and the rest is insurmountable. There are no upsets in the FA Cup any more. Can anyone imagine Manchester United losing to Bournemouth now? Or Arsenal to Yeovil Town? Leeds United to Colchester United? Coventry City to Sutton United? It doesn't happen any more, and it's all down to television.

To many people the football-watching experience involves a big screen and a pint of lager. You can even do it at football grounds now, in the curious bridge between the live and the televisual experience I found at White Hart Lane. These people are no longer fans, they truly are consumers. As Charlton MD Peter Varney told me when we met at The Valley, football clubs look at their supporters as customers now. We are a clientele, not a fanbase. Are those of us who actually go to the matches now a minority?

I finish my pint and leave the Coach and Horses. The FA Cup semi-final advert chalked up on the wall has already been erased and the next attraction is being written in its place. Remind me to throw the television out of the window when I get home. Harrumph.

187